Frisbee Dogs

HOW TO RAISE, TRAIN AND COMPETE

By Peter Bloeme, World Frisbee Champion

PRB & Associates • Atlanta, Georgia

ISBN 0-9629346-2-3

First Edition/First Printing August 1991
Second Edition/Second Printing April 1994

Library of Congress Catalog Card Number: 94-92094

To order additional copies of this book, contact the publisher: PRB & Associates, 4060–D Peachtree Road, Suite 326B, Atlanta, Georgia 30319, (404) 231-9240

Production Notes
This book was produced entirely on the desktop with Macintosh computers using the following software and hardware: QuarkXPress, ColorStudio, LetraStudio, Photoshop, Painter, LaserWriter Pro, Microtek ScanMaker II and 35T.

Contents

A neighborhood dog dives in a San Francisco fountain to keep cool.

This book would not have been possible without the people and organizations listed below. Some contributed more than others but everyone's help was greatly appreciated: Frank Allen, Jeremy Angel, Ashley Whippet, Ian Awbrey, Chris Barbo, Laurie Berkin, Jackie Bernard, Reese Blake, Allyn Rice Bloeme, Erik Borg, Tad Bowen, Esther Branch, Chris Breit, Craig Brownell, Abby Burton, Jeff Carlick, Chronicle Features, Forest Clayton, Barbara Cohen, Cohen & Company, Karl Cook, Bob Cox, Delta Air Lines, Charles Duran, Joanne Duran, Robin Duran, Earle Palmer Brown, Ron Ellis, Bob & Marilyn Evans, Tony Frediani, Friskies Dog Food, Lynne Frye, Jeff Gabel, Paul Gebauer, John Gentry, Gary Gomes, Ken Gorman, Rick Guebert, Terri Hanson, Jeff Hartshorne, Herb Hennigan, Florence Hill, Richard Hill, Mary Hall, Melissa Heeter, Bernie Holmes, Jendi Holmes, Dave Huffine, Hyper Hank, Tia Joslin D.V.M., Henry Khoo, Karen Knox, Robert Knox, Brian Lamky, Irv Lander, Gary Larson, Bethe Lehman, David Letterman, Long Photography, Inc., Brenda Maceo, Marvelous Magic, Walt Mancini, Lou McCammon, Eldon McIntire, Glenn Medford, Dave Menor, Devon Meyers, Chuck Middleton, Eric Miller, Kathy Miller, Mike Miller, John Misita, Betty Moore, Cynthia Mullennix, Richard Munger, Bill Murphy, National Enquirer, Tom Nebbia, Jackie Nickerson, Glenn Osaki, Robert Ozankan, Cheryl Padgett, Jeff Perry, Ken Pogson, Glenn Provenzano, J.P. Rees, Judy Rees, David Robinson, Dan Roddick, Job Sargent, Larry Schindel, Donna Schoech, Stan Sellers, Mike Smith, Alex Stein, Susan Summers, Jennifer Stumpf, Gary Suzuki, Larry Taylor, Time Magazine, Greg Tresan, Phil Van Tee, Beth Wagner, Don Wakefield, Bill Watters, Steve Willett, Whirlin' Wizard, Valdo Williams, Wolf Camera, Mark Wood, Tomiko Yamamoto, Ed Zinn and my wife Lynn Duran

"Catch that for me, won't you Chauncy?"

PHIL VAN TEE

1989 World Champion Gilbert in Berlin, Germany.

Foreword

t's very entertaining to see dogs soaring through the air to catch flying discs, but Frisbee dogs don't just miraculously develop overnight. Training even the most adaptable breeds, like Australian Shepherds, Border Collies and Labrador Retrievers, requires dedication and patience to achieve gratifying results.

When Peter Bloeme asked me to write a foreword for this book, I was flattered. As co-founder and Executive Director of the Ashley Whippet Invitational, along with my 10-year stint as Vice President and member of the Board of Directors of the Los Angeles Society for the Prevention of Cruelty to Animals, I have seen many newspaper articles and books written about Frisbee play and dog training. Many writers, in an attempt to be cute or funny, have not taken the subject seriously. Bloeme has worked long and hard to achieve personal success and professional stature by being a pioneer in the sport, a world champion, a professional performer, a national judge, a world-class dog trainer and now Director of the Friskies Canine Frisbee disc Championships. He takes disc sports seriously, which is why you'll find the material in this book authoritative and sincere.

In any event, I received the invitation to set the tone of this truly excellent and comprehensive work on the care and training of a Frisbee dog with much enthusiasm. Bloeme sets high standards of perfection for himself and others.

Is the book timely? Does it fill a need? Emphatically, **yes!** The national interest in

Cheryl Padgett's alert Aussies.

acquiring and training a dog to be adept at catching a Frisbee disc is at an all-time high thanks to the exploits of high-flying canines on television and in the print media.

Individuals who now own an untrained dog, or who plan to acquire one, will benefit greatly from this book. Bloeme shares with the reader his many experiences as a gifted athlete and the methods he used to train the undefeated 1984 World Champion Whirlin' Wizard, his beloved Border Collie. And Bloeme does it in a down-to-earth, narrative style that, while factual and logical, makes for fascinating reading. Although, it may be true that every expert is not necessarily a good teacher, Bloeme is the real thing. He gives you practical step-by-step guidance, not theory, with his uncanny knack for making complex things seem simple.

Reading this book in manuscript form, I became even more aware of Bloeme's greatest asset: perseverance. Without perseverance in the pursuit of learning and excellence, one will not achieve success to the desired degree. The key is there for you in this book, but you must not be impatient or give up along the way.

Many people have told me they were inspired to procure and train a Frisbee dog after seeing Bloeme perform with Wizard on television or in a stadium. Now they, and you, can intimately share his unique repertoire of tricks by owning this book and by reading and re-reading it thoroughly.

If you're serious about raising and training a Frisbee dog, and becoming a skilled thrower as well, this book by Peter Bloeme is a *must*. Like Bloeme it is World Class in every respect.

Irv Lander
Executive Director,
Friskies Canine Frisbee disc
Championships
aka: The Ashley Whippet
Invitational

WALT MANCINI

Alex Stein & Ashley Whippet III and Irv Lander & Ashley Whippet II.

Introduction

Why teach your canine to play with a Frisbee disc? There are many reasons. Frisbee play is a fantastic way to keep your dog in excellent condition. The running and jumping involved will increase your pet's stamina and improve its muscular strength.

Also, learning to throw a disc and teaching your dog to play will be a challenge for both of you. It offers an opportunity for you and your canine to work together as a team. The camaraderie that you develop with your pet creates a special bond of friendship and gives your dog a special reason for living.

If you decide to compete, you can involve the whole family. Frisbee disc competitions are open to all dogs (and people) regardless of breeding and size. Pound puppies can compete *paw-to-paw* with purebred canines. In fact, many shelter adoptees have gone on to win the World Championship.

Still, the most basic reason for teaching your canine to play is simply that dogs love it!

You may not have a world champion on your hands, but if you read this book carefully and follow the instructions outlined, I'm sure that you will have your dog running, jumping and catching in no time, while providing endless moments of enjoyment to both of you.

JEFF PERRY

1984 World Champions, Wizard and Peter Bloeme, with puppy Magic.

1

How this Book is Organized

The primary focus of this book is on training your dog to play with a Frisbee disc, yet, I am often asked how I became involved in disc sports and what it was like to do various professional shows. Therefore, I have also included this personal information. I hope that by doing so, you will be entertained and perhaps learn something from my experiences.

Some Personal Thoughts

I found that once I began writing about discs and dogs, I wanted to include so much material on raising and training a dog to a world class level that things quickly got out of hand. In order to to cover the topic in a unique, adaptable and useful manner, I concentrated on the areas that I felt to be the most valuable to the typical dog owner. I recommend that you combine the guidance in this book with the resources listed in the Appendix for the best results.

After beginning work on the original manuscript, I realized I wanted another dog. My world champion dog, Whirlin' Wizard was, at the time of that writing, 8 years old and deserved to retire from the daily routine of performing. Having a puppy to practice with while writing a book on training a dog is certainly advantageous, so it was easy to justify to myself (and to my wife) the addition of a new pup. I purchased an 11-week-old Australian Shepherd, and named him Magic. He looks a lot like Wizard minus a long tail with which to sweep off the coffee table. The third day I had him we traveled to Dallas, Texas, where I appeared as a member of the Friskies Celebrity Touring Team. While there, Magic made his first appearance on NBC television chasing a disc. Since then he has been catching in Wizard's *pawsteps*.

Casey doing some required reading.

The first version of Frisbee Dogs has been extremely popular and well received with thousands of books sold. In this revision, I have tried to answer readers questions, elaborate in some areas, update information where appropriate, add additional pages and enhance the quality of the photos, paper and type.

To eliminate possible confusion and to make writing easier, I will, for the most part, use male pronouns when I refer to all dogs unless I know they are female. Both my dogs are male, therefore it is more natural for me to use a masculine reference.

As you pursue this activity and work with your pet, please feel free to write me with your discoveries and insights. I welcome your comments and new ideas as the great sport of canine Frisbee play continues to grow, develop and evolve.

Write to: **Peter Bloeme**

PRB & Associates
4060-D Peachtree Road, Suite 326B
Atlanta, Georgia 30319

Nine Poodle pups born to Frisbee dog father Bentley, owned by Judy and JP Rees.

3

Don Wakefield and Carbo dazzle spectators at the LA County Fairgrounds.

Frisbee History

Most people who become involved with Frisbee dogs are led to the sport by their canines and are usually unaware of its early history. Other people (like myself), enter the sport through disc sports. Either way, the history of the disc is quite interesting and certainly worth knowing.

In 1871, a man named William Russell Frisbie settled in Bridgeport, Connecticut and took over the management of a new bakery. Soon after, he bought it outright and renamed it *The Frisbie Pie Company*. At its peak it turned out more than 80,000 pies per day!

Of the Frisbee brand flying disc, Gay Talese of the *New York Times* wrote on August 11, 1957:

"Possibly the name is used in recognition of the Frisbie Baking Company of Bridgeport, Connecticut, which after World War II had a clientele notoriously famous for not returning tin pie plates.

'Somebody discovered a pie-plate-pitching game and it was found that our tin plates were excellent for scaling (throwing),' a company official said. 'During that fad we lost about 5,000 tin pie plates.'"

Two weeks later, on August 25, 1957, the Times published the following letter:

"...It is common knowledge in New Haven that Frisbie has been played at Yale for over a century...at Yale, birthplace of the sport, Frisbie is a heritage—a whole way of life."

Credit for the development

Frisbie Pie Tin.

is a heritage—a whole way of life."

Credit for the development of the modern plastic product can be given to Walter Fred Morrison, whose father invented the sealed-beam auto headlight. In 1947 Morrison carved the first flying disc from a block of tenite (an early plastic). He soon found that tenite was too brittle, so in 1948 he used a plastic that could be molded.

According to Dr. Stancil E.D. Johnson in his book, *Frisbee, "This original Morrison's Flyin' Saucer was his Arcuate Vane Model, named for the six topside (flight plate) curved spoilers (vanes)...Curiously, the spoilers were on backward; that is, they would theoretically work only for a counterclockwise spin."* That disc was the predecessor of today's Frisbee discs.

In late 1955, Wham-O Manufacturing Company (hereafter simply referred to as Wham-O) founders, Rich Knerr and A.K. *Spud* Melin (who started their company in a garage where they produced sling shots), saw the *Pluto Platter* (Morrison's revised *Arcuate Vane*) and liked the product so much that they purchased the rights to manu-

ERIK BORG/TIME MAGAZINE

Frisbee dog statue in Milford, Connecticut by Patrick Villers Farrow.

Ashley Whippet Jr flips in photo shoot for National Geographic Magazine.

facture and sell it.

On January 13, 1957 the first Pluto Platter rolled off the Wham-O production line; in 1958 the Frisbie Pie Company went out of business, signalling the end of one era and the beginning of another.

Dr. Johnson also wrote in his book *Frisbee:*

"On a trip to the campuses of the Ivy League, Knerr first heard the term 'frisbie.' Harvard students said they'd tossed pie tins around for years and called it frisbieing. Knerr liked the terms frisbie and frisbieing, so he borrowed them. Having no idea of the historical origins, he spelled the saucer Frisbee, phonetically correct, but one vowel away from the Frisbie Pie Company."

And in the May 1975 edition of *Oui Magazine*, James R. Petersen wrote:

"To avoid legal trouble with the Frisbie Pie Company, Fred Morrison changed the ie to ee and patented the Frisbee Flying Disk [sic]. It was a cosmic example of name it and claim it. Like Kleenex, like Xerox, Frisbee became the noun for all varieties of the product. Unlike Kleenex, like Xerox, Frisbee also became a verb and a way of life."

On May 26, 1959, Wham-O was granted a registered trademark on the word *Frisbee*. It is trademark number 679,186 for *"Toy flying saucers for toss games."* Called everything from disc, to disk, to sport

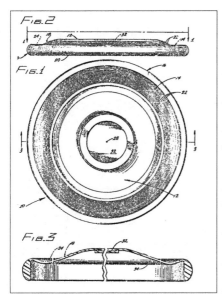

The figure at left is a Wham-O patent drawing of the Fastback Frisbee disc. This text is from the patent description.

"Over the past decade, toys resembling inverted platters or saucers have enjoyed great popularity as recreational items for use in throwing games and contests. In the usual embodiment the toy is made of a plastic material in a circular configuration with a rim portion located at its periphery, the rim portion being relatively thick in comparison to the remaining portions of the implement. In its normal inverted platter orientation, the rim curves downwardly from the toy body giving the implement a shape which approximates that of an airfoil when viewed in elevation. Such a toy has been marketed for the period indicated above by the assignee of the present application under the trademark Frisbee."

7

1993 World Runners-up Herb Hennigan and Cow Dog.

disc, to flying disc, to flying saucer, there has never been a more widely accepted name for this product than the original term Frisbee (Frisbee disc by Wham-O), which has been used now for more than 30 years.

The meaning behind the word Frisbee transcends the flying disc. It is, and has always been both, a sport and a way of life. Since its first use as a pie tin, this *toy* became a fad, turned into a game, then sport, and took off in popularity. Disc play has gained respectability; today it's taught and played in many schools and universities. There is now a World Flying Disc Federation based in Sweden with 26 member nations as well as a number of contests, mail order businesses and publications devoted to this world class sport.

Close up view of the Fastback Frisbee disc by Wham-O.

Three-time World Champion Ashley Whippet flies over Malibu Beach.

Canine History

No one actually knows the identity of the first person to throw a disc to his or her dog, but the credit for popularizing this activity must go to Alex Stein, owner and trainer of the legendary three-time world canine Frisbee disc champion, Ashley Whippet. Besides being his registered name, Ashley actually was a Whippet; a breed that looks like a small Greyhound—sleek, smooth, short-haired, athletic and very fast.

Ashley was born in Oxford, Ohio on October 2, 1971. Stein received him as a gift and took him everywhere. He soon discovered that he had no ordinary run-of-the-mill dog! Ashley would chase, leap, spin in the air and catch just about any disc thrown (which at the time were large Super Pro Frisbee discs).

Stein had the intuition that Ashley could make it in show business, so he boldly moved from Cleveland, Ohio to Hollywood, California; the land of opportunity for the unusual.

When he called the various talent agencies, he told them he had a dog that ran 35 miles-per-hour, jumped nine feet, spun in the air and caught flying discs. They answered, *"You have a dog that can run how fast, jump how high and catch what?"* then hung up. But Stein didn't give up; he approached Wham-O, the maker of Frisbee discs.

At first, Wham-O showed little interest, so Stein dreamed up a way to attract their attention. He wanted to show that Ashley was attention-grab-

Ashley Whippet Jr. jumps for joy in Berlin, Germany while Alex Stein assists.

11

bing, exciting, newsworthy and entertaining. Fortunately for the sport, both Stein and Ashley had great courage, talent and determination.

So in August of 1974, Stein smuggled Ashley into Dodger Stadium during a nationally televised baseball game. Between the seventh and eighth innings, the duo ran onto the field and performed for eight minutes before Stein was arrested. Their debut almost turned catastrophic when, during the arrest, Ashley disappeared. Irv Lander, then Director of the International Frisbee Association, happened to be at the game and bailed Stein out of jail. For three days, both men were sick with worry at the thought that Ashley might be lost forever. Fortunately, a boy who had seen the performance found Ashley roaming the stadium parking lot, took him home and cared for him until his parents could get in touch with Stein.

The crowd loved the impromptu show which brought the pair national publicity. Since that memorable baseball game, Stein and Ashley have become legendary among Frisbee aficionados, performing at Super Bowl XII, *The Tonight Show, Merv Griffin, Late Night*

Alex Stein and Ashley Whippet entertained thousands at football game halftimes.

with David Letterman and even at the White House for Amy Carter. Then, when competition began for canines, Ashley ran away with three world titles.

Why Ashley was so talented no one knows. Whippets, in general, are not renowned Frisbee dogs. Still, I have never seen a dog more beautiful and graceful,

Alex Stein at his "Deli on Rye" in Hudson, Ohio.

as fast or as high a leaper as Ashley was.

After an action packed life of entertaining millions and popularizing an exciting activity for owners and their dogs, Ashley Whippet passed away on March 11, 1985 at the age of 14.

In his lifetime, Ashley set the standards for the sport. Yet he was just the beginning. People often ask me who is, or was, the greatest Frisbee dog. I can't compare Ashley or other great dogs of the past with the champions of today because of the sport's rapid growth and development. New tricks, rules and training methods have all added variables that make comparisons impossible.

Alex Stein toured for a number of years with Ashley's pups, Ashley Jr, Ashley III and Lady Ashley as a member of the Ashley Whippet Invitational Celebrity Touring Team and Chief Judge. Recently he settled down, got married and opened Deli on Rye in Hudson, Ohio (south of Cleveland). If you're in the area, be sure to stop by. The food is excellent and there is no better story teller of the days of old than Stein who is always serving up another one.

Another popular team deserving credit for making the sport what it is today, is Eldon McIntire and his Australian Shepherd, Hyper Hank. They rank high in the annals of canine Frisbee history, and few dogs are as aptly named. Hyper Hank perfectly complemented Ashley Whippet. Ashley was small, sleek and mellow; Hank was large, hairy and excitable hence the name Hyper. He would run through a wall to catch a disc. McIntire and Hyper Hank frequently toured with Stein and Ashley. Their many historic canine Frisbee performances together included performances at the Super Bowl and at the White House.

13

WALT MANCINI

WALT MANCINI

Ashley Whippet soars skyward as pal Hyper Hank watches in amazement.

Lady Ashley, daughter of Ashley Whippet, shows off her form.

WHITE HOUSE

Amy Carter throws to Ashley Whippet on the White House lawn in 1977 while Irv Lander (left), Alex Stein (second from right) and a friend watch.

Eldon McIntire and Hyper Hank were early innovators of the sport.

Although the dogs themselves frequently get the accolades (and rightfully so), we would not be where we are today without the incredible dedication, drive, energy and support of Irv Lander, who has always been a dog lover.

After seeing these great dogs perform, Lander felt that an opportunity existed to provide a sponsor with an attention grabbing event and dog lovers with an exciting sport. A competition would serve many purposes. For a sponsor, it would provide a unique promotional opportunity. For dog owners, it would physically challenge them to learn new throws, tricks and techniques. For dogs it would provide great exercise and an opportunity to compete as a team with their owner.

Lander, who had worked closely for many years with the Society for the Prevention of Cruelty to Animals (SPCA) in Los Angeles, felt that an additional side benefit from the sport of canine Frisbee would be to encourage people to adopt pets from shelters.

In the beginning, the contest was held in conjunction with the World Frisbee Championships at the Rose Bowl. With the support of a corporate sponsor, Lander was able to redesign the event so that it could stand on its own.

Lander made many sacrifices to establish the sport. He worked on a shoestring budget the first few years, staying in flea-bag motels while

THE
ASHLEY WHIPPET
INVITATIONAL WORLD
CANINE FRISBEE
CHAMPIONSHIPS

1984 PETER BLOEME "WHIRLIN' WIZARD"	1987 JEFF GABEL "CASEY"	1990
1985 BILL MURPHY "BOUNCIN' BOO"	1988 JEFF GABEL "CASEY"	1991
1986 CHRIS BARBO "KATO"	1989 JEFF PERRY "GILBERT"	1992

The three foot tall "Lander Cup" features the engraved names of all the World Champions and their dogs

Eldon McIntire.

on the road, and spent a great deal of his personal savings in order to ensure the contest's success.

Lander's hard work and sacrifice over the years has resulted in a contest that provides a sponsor with a nationally-known, promotional tie-in. The dogs make the contest a family-oriented media event, free to the public and a great time for all.

In honor of Lander's efforts, the members of the 1990 Friskies Celebrity Touring Team created the *Lander Cup.* This new symbol for the sport is similar to hockey's *Stanley Cup* and lists all the world champions in the sport. It is displayed in the office of the Friskies Canine Frisbee disc Championships.

Because of the efforts of Stein, Lander, McIntire and more recent staff members such as 1989 World Champion Jeff Perry and myself, Frisbee dogs have become a national pastime and the sport is spreading across the world with exhibitions and contests throughout Europe and Asia.

Eldon McIntire and Hyper Hank entertain Amy Carter on the White House lawn.

17

Eldon McIntire and Cricket practicing for a Friskies television commercial in Furano, Japan.

Peter Bloeme/Wizard/Magic

The first two chapters of this book have set the stage with information on the history of the flying disc and canine Frisbee. My involvement in flying disc sports ran a parallel path on the human side to Alex Stein and Ashley Whippet's.

I still remember the first day I threw a Frisbee disc. When I was twelve years old in 1968, my cousin Lynne and her boyfriend Moose took me to Central Park in New York City. While Lynne watched, Moose attempted to teach me how to play with a Frisbee disc. As many people do at first, I threw it a long distance, but not in the direction I was aiming. Moose seemed frustrated by constantly having to run after my throws, but I was hooked, and disc sports became my new challenge.

About a year later while walking through Central Park, my friend Job Sargent and I saw some people (who back then were called *hippies*) playing with a Frisbee disc. We wanted to join in their game but were too shy to ask. We waited, hoping a wild throw would come our way and eventually, one did. I ran after it and threw it back. After this happened a few times, they asked us if we wanted to join them. Both Sargent and I did, and we went on to discover that people gathered at that spot every day to socialize and play disc sports. From that point on, we went there every chance we had. It was not an area especially well suited for playing: the field was small—about 30 yards long and 40 yards wide, and because of a gradual slope on one end that dropped down to Central Park's row-boat lake, it was known as *Frisbee Hill.*

The daily scene consisted of informal groups: *throwers, middle-men,* and

Peter Bloeme at 15 years of age.

chasers. Throwers stayed at the top of the hill and threw Frisbee discs down to the *chasers,* while the *middle men* threw to each other.

Whenever the two best throwers on the hill, Jim and Mel, challenged each other to a *hill throw* (a term used to describe how far they could throw the Frisbee disc), everything stopped. It was a beautiful sight, watching the discs gently curve over and then down the hill. As *chasers,* Sargent and I would follow the discs, try to make catches and relay them back. I credit my unusual, but successful, long distance throwing style to being a *chaser.* It took a different technique to throw up the hill, and as time passed, I could return those *hill throws* all the way from the bottom. Occasionally, for variety, we joined the *middle men* to work on trick throws and catches.

Since nearly everyone I played disc sports with was older than me, I didn't realize how good I was for my own age until I entered the Junior Frisbee disc Tournament in 1972. Designed for children 15 years old and under, it was hosted nationwide by local parks and recreation departments and was sponsored by Wham-O.

In my first distance event I threw a Frisbee disc 90 yards: not only did the throw surpass the 60-yard scoring maximum, but the disc continued to fly over the recreation building at the end of the field, astonishing the officials.

I went on to win the city, state and then regional championships. As the east coast champion, I won free airline tickets for myself and

JACKIE NICKERSON

Peter Bloeme at ages 15, 19 and 28 performing the same behind-the-back catch.

an adult chaperon to the National Junior Frisbee Finals in Las Vegas, Nevada. I chose my coach and friend, Valdo Williams, a professional jazz pianist and karate expert, to accompany me. Williams, whom I had met in the park, became a father figure to me over the years, as my own father passed on when I was 10. Williams and I spent much of our free time playing disc sports together. The fact that he did not drink or use drugs made Williams a very positive influence on those around him.

Valdo Williams.

I finished third overall at the Nationals and first in distance out of more than one and a half million junior competitors from all over the United States. It was there that I first met Irv Lander, then the National Junior Frisbee Contest Director. After the tournament, I wrote him a letter thanking him for running the contest in a professional and smooth manner. In return, I received an unexpected and memorable reply. He wrote:

"...Although you did not achieve your goal this time, you were far and away the most spectacular Frisbee performer in the history of our National Junior Frisbee Championships.

"Surely there will be many additional honors that your skills and dedication will earn for you in the future. I am certain that your name will be prominent in adult Frisbee competition for years to come...."

Since then, Lander has been a great influence on my personal and professional life, and working with him is always a pleasure and an honor. Lander, because of his love for Ashley and the sport of canine Frisbee, became the executive director for the Ashley Whippet Invitational and is, primarily responsible for the organized sport as it exists today.

In 1975, I earned my World Class Masters rating (disc sport's highest) by successfully completing the International Frisbee Association's proficiency test, which required many assorted throws and catches. It took place at the World Frisbee Championships (WFC) in the famed Rose Bowl in Pasadena, California.

In 1976 I practiced ardently for several hours every day. Early in the season at the Eastern National Championships, known as *Octad,* I set a short-lived world record in Throw, Run and Catch (TRC), an event that measures the distance a person runs between his throw and his catch (my TRC was 213 feet). More importantly, I won the Eastern National Overall title. Later that year, I went to Boston and won the Eastern National Distance title and came close to setting another world record.

Before the tournament, the world distance record was 366 feet. I finished with a throw of 375 feet! No one can say how much farther my throw would have gone had it not been stopped cold by a fence. Unfortunately, I was a day too late to set the world record, because on the previous day in the semi-finals, Dave Johnson, a tall, thin and very powerful man, made a throw of 412 feet!

By doing well at those two tournaments I earned another invitation to the World Frisbee Championships at the Rose Bowl. This was the beginning of a much tougher tournament format. To win the overall, one had to score well in six events versus the previous two events, distance and accuracy. I competed against more than 100 of the top disc sports players from around the world. All the front runners started strong, but after the second day the field narrowed, and by the third day it was a race between John Kirkland, a college professor from Boston, and myself, with accuracy as the deciding event.

Kirkland approached me the evening before the accuracy event. He told me that he was going to beat me and win the overall title. I have to admit that I was a little intimidated because accuracy had

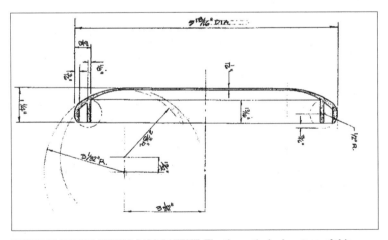

PETER BLOEME'S FLYING DISC PATENT: The theoretical advantage of this design over others is that there is more mass along the edge which should improve distance thrown. Additionally, the inner rim provides a better gripping surface which would allow greater control of throws.

always been my weakest event. I knew that he expected me to choke; instead, his boastful comments gave me the motivation I needed to really concentrate. That night, I planned my strategy, and since I wanted to remain focused, I cancelled my scheduled morning television appearance on *The Mickey Mouse Show*. I wanted to throw early in the day, when the weather was calm and I would have no distractions as Kirkland would be away at the television show.

In the morning the weather was clear, allowing me to compete under ideal conditions for accuracy. When Kirkland arrived in the afternoon, he asked me how I had done. When I told him my score of 16 out of 28 (my best ever), I think it caused **him** to choke. Ironically, on the final day, I not only won the world accuracy title but the Men's Overall World Frisbee Champion title as well. UPI (United Press International) wire service reported after the event:

"The contest was destined to be an anticlimax. After all, among the entrants in the World Frisbee Championships was John Kirkland, the Massachusetts Institute of Technology professor who specializes in the physics and aerodynamics of sustained Frisbee flight. He had honed his art to perfection because he found it 'spiritually fulfilling.'

"Once the air had cleared on championship day in Los Angeles, the academic emerged with a firm grip on the prize—for second place. Peter Bloeme, a 19-year-old New York City resident, apparently said nothing profound enough to be quoted. He finished first."

Because I had won two world titles, I was eligible for an endorsement contract with Wham-O, which I gratefully accepted. I considered it more of an honor than a financial jackpot. My name appeared on all their 1977 World Class Model Frisbee discs.

Peter Bloeme demonstrating a difficult freestyle combination.

It was at this championship that I first met and became friends with Alex Stein, the owner of Ashley Whippet. I also mingled with the other Frisbee dog owners who were there to compete in the canine world championships. The dogs' abilities astonished me, and although I loved dogs, I resented their popularity with the media and the public. As a human competitor, I sometimes felt ignored and jealous. The dogs appeared limited to jumping and catching, and it didn't seem fair that I spent hours each day practicing and perfecting technique and style only to receive less attention. Now, of course, because of my involvement in and experience with canine disc play, I feel differently. I believe that Frisbee dogs and their owners have advanced greatly in technique and overall ability since those early days.

The following year, I worked part-time as a Frisbee professional. Occasionally, I worked with Stein throwing long distance throws to Ashley Whippet, which led me to judging local canine Frisbee disc contests.

One of my most unusual competitive experiences took place at the Eastern Accuracy Championship in Tampa, Florida. Everything ran late the second day of the tournament and when we reached the finals of accuracy, it was dark. Some judges and competitors used their cars headlights to illuminate the field so the other finalist and I could see the target. I won in what amounted to total darkness.

In 1978, I concentrated my competitive efforts on playing Ulti-

Peter Bloeme, Alex Stein and Ashley Whippet performing at a racetrack.

mate for Cornell University. (Ultimate is a disc sport that combines elements of soccer, football and basketball and is played on a 40 by 70 yard field with 25 yard end zones and seven person teams.) The club team consisted almost entirely of college players, and though I did not attend Cornell, they invited me to join them. We made it to the finals of the National Ultimate

Peter Bloeme playing Ultimate on the East Coast all-star team at the Rose Bowl in 1977.

Championship against the Santa Barbara Condors (another club team) and finished second in a highly competitive game.

A Frisbee player since 1969, I became a full-time professional in 1978. Since then I have performed hundreds of times throughout the U.S., Canada, Japan, England, Spain, Germany and Sweden. My professional status led to many television commercials, including a spot for Pepsi-Cola, and numerous interviews on both radio and television, including ABC, CBS, CNN, ESPN, and NBC *(see Professional Appearances page 159 for more on these experiences)*. I also created a Frisbee show that I perform at schools, camps, amusement parks, fairs, sport shows, shopping malls and sporting event halftimes. Having amassed a collection of over 3,000 flying discs of all shapes, colors and sizes *(see back cover photo for a partial glimpse)*. I have even designed and patented a high performance flying disc *(see page 22 for drawing)*. Still, my proudest accomplishment is raising and training Whirlin' Wizard, the 1984 World Champion and Hall of Fame Frisbee dog.

Whirlin' Wizard

No matter where I performed as a Frisbee professional, people would always ask me if I had a Frisbee dog. My typical answer was, *"No, I don't. It's just too difficult traveling with one."*

Then, in 1982, on a cross-country drive from Seattle to New York, I pondered additions and changes that I would make in my Frisbee show for the coming season. This is when I first started to think seriously about getting a dog. I *tossed* the idea around, picturing what it would have been like having a dog the previous year. How would my life have been different? Would I have missed out on anything or lived where I did? During the long drive, I had a lot of time to think through those questions and my feelings were positive. I enjoyed the idea of having a dog to travel with and share my life as well as a Frisbee partner to work with. By the time I reached Montana, I had just about decided to get a dog, but had one remaining concern; nutrition. Then, in a motel room I flipped on the television and the Westminster Dog Show came on. I watched as a veterinarian discussed healthy food for dogs. After seeing the show, I became aware that there are many good commercial foods now available for dogs. On the rest of that drive to New York I thought about the specifics of acquiring, training, traveling with and feeding a dog.

My first decision was what breed to select. Because of my travel schedule, I decided not to get a large dog. From my familiarity with Ashley Whippet, I began to research Whippets. I called the American Kennel Club (AKC) in New York City and they gave me the name and telephone number of the secretary of a Whippet club.

When I spoke with her she immediately asked, *"Why are you interested in getting a Whippet?"* I told her I wanted to train one for catching Frisbee. She sounded appalled and asked me how I could think of doing such a thing. She went on to tell me that they were fragile little animals and that one of her dogs had broken a leg just running and playing in the back yard. I restrained myself from mentioning that sometimes physical weaknesses of *purebred* dogs are due to their being bred or inbred solely for their appearance.

Secretly annoyed, I continued by asking her if she had ever heard of Ashley Whippet. She answered *"Of course."* She had seen him perform live and told me she was concerned every time he jumped. Alex Stein, Ashley's owner, laughed when I told him the story. He told me that Ashley had never been injured in the 12 years he competed and performed.

1984 World Champion Wizard at three months of age.

I continued my quest for a dog. After much research, thought and reflection, I selected a Border Collie. The determining factor was seeing three-time World Finalist Jendi Holmes' exciting Border Collies in action.

Border Collies are purebred sheep herding dogs originally from Scotland. Medium-sized dogs bred for intelligence, stamina and obedience, they are usually black and white and are fully recognized as a breed by the International Sheep Dog Association. I especially liked their appearance. Later I discovered that although the sport was founded by Ashley Whippet, he was the exception. On average, Whippets are not particularly good Frisbee dogs.

Once I made up my mind to get a dog to train for disc sports, I noticed an advertisement in *Dog World Magazine*

Eight-month-old Wizard at his first professional show at Shea Stadium in '84.

for three month-old Border Collie pups in Gettysburg, Pennsylvania. While driving to the Pacific Northwest from New York on tour, I stopped to look at them. It was winter and they were outside in a dog house. They didn't seem to mind the cold and were having a grand time jumping on each other, play fighting and rolling around in the snow. There were three males to choose from. The first one saw me and ran away, arguably a smart move on his part, but unacceptable to me as I took it personally. The remaining two were both very friendly. I finally chose the smaller one because he was less aggressive, yet very responsive, bright eyed and bushy tailed.

I named him Whirlin' Wizard and he use to think he had it easy—his job was just to *herd* Frisbee discs. I kidded him now and then that he should appreciate me or I would make him get a real job, with lots of sheep.

From the first day, Wizard was a delight. He started out as a little soft, fluffy pup with what looked like huge nuclear-powered paws. He is now a retired World Class, World Champion and Hall of Fame Frisbee dog. Audiences only saw the result of our efforts and commented on his amazing abilities. What they didn't realize was how much practice time was involved.

I began to train Wizard immediately by feeding him out of a disc,

27

which I still do. He caught his first Mini-Frisbee disc, about three inches in diameter, at 14 weeks. At that age, I didn't want to use a full-sized disc and take the chance of damaging his teeth or knocking his head off. I added Wizard to my professional Frisbee shows when he was just 16 weeks old.

At the age of 8 months, Wizard made his professional sporting debut at Shea Stadium between games of a double header for the New York Mets (vs. Philadelphia Phillies) with over 40,000 spectators. He performed like a true professional. We probably didn't make a big *hit* with the New York Mets until after the performance, because Wizard got sick before the show in one of their offices. As I cleaned it up, I realized he must have been a little nervous.

Wizard never had any *formal* obedience training but, as a foundation for all of his Frisbee stunts I taught him all the standard commands: sit, stay, down, heel. He learned to obey through both voice and hand signals, making him, in a way, bilingual. When he was a pup, I worked with him four times a day for 15 minutes at a time. Before his retirement, we worked about 30 minutes a day—every day, whether it was raining, snowing or sunny. The reason for practicing in all types of weather conditions is that I never knew if we would be required to perform or compete in less than ideal conditions. At one canine world finals, for example, a recent rain shower left the ground wet. One of the top dogs there that day didn't perform to her potential because she didn't like the wet ground.

Peter Bloeme makes a long throw to Wizard at a Washington Redskin's football halftime.

Associated Press sports feature award-winning photograph by Jeff Carlick:
1984 World Champions Peter Bloeme and Whirlin' Wizard.

JACKIE BERNARD

1984 World Champion Whirlin' Wizard.

Wizard still considers playing with Frisbee discs fun. All I have to do is say the word *"Frisbee"* and his ears perk up, his head tilts sideways and he stands motionless. Or as Delta Air Lines' Cynthia Mullennix put it in her feature article in Delta Dispatch, *"Wizard comes as close to smiling as a dog can."* When I pick up a Frisbee disc or even a ball, stick or other toy, he crouches down and stares at the object. Believe it or not, this means he's ready to play. The hard work for me came in channeling this excitement and energy into his becoming a top competitor and performer.

One drawback of owning a sheep-herding dog is the amount of exercise required to keep him happy. In his younger days if Wizard didn't get a good workout every day he would drive himself and anyone else around crazy by trying to get volunteers to play with him. This breed simply has a ton of energy. Some dogs chew on an old shoe. Sheep dogs start chewing at one end of a couch and finish at the other. Some dogs dig holes, but sheep dogs excavate! In fact, my current performing dog, Magic, is working to link-up the Eurotunnel with our backyard.

Some weekends when I played the flying disc game Ultimate, my team might play three games. Naturally, before, during halftime and after each game, Wizard ran wild on the field seeking any human willing to throw him his beloved toy. It was quite a sight to see one dog amid 20 players running, jumping, catching and seemingly never tiring. Yet, by the end of the day when we got in the car, he would lie down and immediately go to sleep. When we got home he would pull himself together stiffly, stagger up the stairs and plop down in his favorite spot. Just when I started to think that taking him to Ultimate was a great way of tiring him out, he would push one of his toys onto my feet and crouch eagerly, expecting me to play. Amazing!

One of our most memorable experiences took place at an elementary school. Wizard is very obedient, except he doesn't always obey the command *"Stay."* He loves Frisbee discs and children too much plus he knew that in the middle of my show I wouldn't be able to correct him properly. So after he performed, I would put his leash on him and look for someone to hold onto him for the remainder of my show.

At this elementary school, when it was time to find someone to hold him, I turned around and asked the closest adult (who happened to be the principal) to hold Wizard. Actually, I didn't ask but just walked over and handed him Wizard's leash and continued my presentation. I didn't know why at the time, but many of the adults, teachers and parents, laughed. After the first show, the PTO (Parent Teacher Organization) president told me the reason for the laughter—the principal was afraid of dogs, so I made a mental note not to pick him during the next show.

Imagine my surprise during the second show when I turned to look for an adult to hold Wizard the same principal came running up and took him. After the demonstration he spoke to me at length. It turned out that he had a daughter who loved animals and he was considering getting her a dog, possibly a Border Collie, all because of Wizard.

One of the most frequently asked questions is, *"How long did it take to teach Wizard?"* Because Wizard knows so much, I have to ask, *"Teach him what?"* It took different amounts of time to learn every trick he knows, and he is always learning. I answer by giving his present age and explain that he is continuously working on new things. Every day I try to find something new to challenge him. For example, once I put his favorite basketball in my rope hammock. After a bit of coaching and practice he learned how to bounce it out from the middle, not an easy task from a dog's perspective.

Ashley's Hall of Fame Award: Presented to undefeated World Champions Peter Bloeme and Whirlin' Wizard for their achievement in competition and invaluable contributions to the sport of K-9 Frisbee (1988).

Marvelous Magic

Working with Magic over the past three years has been a real education and sometimes a humbling experience. I went from Wizard, who you could just about ask to read a training book—to Magic who would just as soon eat the training book. I went through choke collars, pinch collars and leashes with his basic obedience training. From chewing to aggression and lack of attention, Marvelous Magic was first known to me as Maniac Magic.

Many of my problems were simply caused by the fact that Wizard got my full attention whereas with Magic, I have had to divide my attention between two dogs, two cats and a wife. Working with Magic taught me a great lesson and hopefully made the material in this book more practical. **Like children, each dog is different and requires a modification of one's training methods.** Patience and hard work plus discovering and developing your dogs natural abilities and tendencies will pay off with a successful and happy Frisbee dog.

Now that I have provided some background information on myself, Wizard and Magic, it is time to look into some of the considerations one needs to take into account before acquiring a dog and teaching him to catch a Frisbee disc.

Magic with one of his "close" relatives.

Peter Bloeme and Marvelous Magic on the Mall in Washington, D.C.

JEFF PERRY

World Finalist and Hall of Famer Donna Schoech and Charity.

Key Canine Considerations

There are few things that disgust me as much as puppy mills where sick, mistreated and malnourished dogs are bred for profit to fill pet store windows.

Buying or adopting a dog should not be done on impulse. If acquiring a puppy, you can expect to spend 15 years, or more, with your friend. Do not get a dog because of a passing fancy, popular movie or simply to placate your children.

Acquiring a dog is a big responsibility and a puppy needs constant care and attention. **Never** give a dog as a gift without asking the recipient first. It is incredibly sad to see dog shelters swell soon after the holiday season with pups that were given as presents who then outgrew their cuteness.

Keep in mind that your dog will depend on you for shelter, health care, food, entertainment and love for his lifetime. Despite those responsibilities, I believe the effort is well worth the love, dedication, loyalty, companionship and protection received in return.

I found it interesting that when I started making appearances and performing in Japan I was asked if I would sell Frisbee dogs. I never have nor ever will sell a *Frisbee dog*. Frisbee dogs are not sold but rather developed along with their owners. It is a team sport. A great thrower or a great dog by himself is nothing. Don't think you need to acquire a pup from a litter of accomplished Frisbee Dogs either. Frisbee ability is a trained skill, not genetic.

Selecting a Dog

Each pure breed and mixed breed has different physical characteristics, inherited qualities and

Atlanta Dog & Disc Club member Olive.

weaknesses such as size, intelligence, speed, stamina, agility, jumping ability and intensity. Pure breeds with long snouts and long legs, such as German Shepherds, Labrador Retrievers and Border Collies, have a better chance of catching a flying disc than snub-nosed dogs or toy breeds which are not well suited to Frisbee play because of their physical limitations. Other elements should be considered: Do you have children, need a dog for protection or simply have preferences for one breed or another? Once you make a selection, part of your responsibility as a dog owner and trainer is to learn to recognize and work with your dog's particular characteristics and special qualities. For example, a hound will be a great tracker, a working dog will be tireless, a hunter will be focused, etc. A good book for investigating various pure breeds is *Simon & Schuster's Guide To Dogs,* listed in the Appendix.

Purebred dogs can be found through advertisements in your local newspaper, or through magazines such as *Dog World* and *Dog Fancy* and even at animal shelters. If you decide to select one of these, I recommend that you also buy some books on the breed you select. They contain useful information from which you will certainly benefit.

Perhaps you might consider adopting a wonderful dog from an

animal shelter like John Misita did with CJ. CJ has developed (or more likely has developed John) into a World Finalist. Most shelters offer beautiful dogs for little or no money. The all-American mutt can be a great selection as long as he has the physical characteristics necessary for the sport. To date, five former World Canine Frisbee Champions were rescued from the pound. With the many unwanted dogs available, saving a dog from the pound can be an especially rewarding experience.

Immediately after acquiring a new dog, get him a collar with the proper identification imprinted including his name, your name, address and tele-

World Finalists CJ and John Misita.

phone number. Have him wear the collar at **all** times, even in the house. If, by accident, you become separated from your dog, an identification tag could be a lifesaver. As collars can come off by themselves and can be taken off, you might consider getting your dog an identification tattoo. Check with your veterinarian on this.

Early exposure to Frisbee is one thing but this is ridiculous!

Health

When you get a dog, make sure that he is healthy, lively, friendly and energetic. Before selecting a purebred, research that breed at your public library or local book store. The information available should inform you of any health-related concerns.

Since it is imperative that your dog be healthy before attempting any strenuous Frisbee activity, check with your veterinarian before starting out. Have your pet examined regularly. Keep your dog dewormed, heartworm free and keep all his immunizations (such as rabies, parvo, kennel cough) current. Remember, your dog can't tell you if he isn't feeling well, so you must develop the ability to asses his physical and mental condition. Learn to be observant. Notice whether or not your dog is eating properly, check his stools for any discharges or worms, inspect for body odor, broken nail/tooth, etc. While petting your dog, you may feel bumps or lacerations, notice unusual hair loss, parasites, etc. These are all warning signs which should be investigated further.

Fleas are a problem, especially in warmer climates, but with baths, dips and bombs they can be controlled. I do not recommend the use of flea collars, though. Think twice before placing a collar around your dog's neck that contains chemicals which, according to the manufacturer, are hazardous to humans. Many veterinarians believe that they may do more harm than good. If you do decide to use one, at least remove the collar when giving your dog a bath or letting him swim. The flea-killing chemicals used are intensified by water and are concentrated around your dog's head. Your money will be better spent on a flea dip or spray.

Teeth

If you begin with a puppy, prepare yourself for the nightmare of **teething.** Take this as a warning: A pup is like an infant and will put everything and anything into his mouth. The difference is that infants don't have pincer-like teeth that can tear cloth, run women's hose, eat one shoe out of every pair in the house and destroy the newspaper better than the government can shred classified information.

What you can do to alleviate the situation is to buy chew-toys (by the gross if necessary), including rubber bones, balls, etc. If you think your dog will like it—get it. However, do not give your dog an old pair of shoes or socks. Think of it this way: How is your dog going to know an old pair of shoes from a favorite new pair? Avoid giving your dog real bones as these can cause severe intestinal blockage or damage due to splintering. Also, be aware that rawhide when chewed til soft, may choke a dog or cause gastrointestinal upset.

Always, keep an eye on your dog when he is chewing. It is easy to assume that your dog is happily chewing something you approve of, only to look down and find out it is not so. The genetic makeup of puppies suggests anything within *mouth range* is fair game. Can we help it if that item happens to be a 220 volt dishwasher cord? The answer is yes, I hope.

Since a pup has baby teeth, do not start throwing any big or hard toys, including regular-sized flying discs, for him to catch until his adult teeth are in which is usually around 6 months. It is important for his puppy teeth to come in and drop out naturally so that the adult teeth grow in normally. Incidentally, your dog's teeth will need to be cleaned by a veterinarian periodically, as dogs can develop gum disease similar to humans. Regular cleanings will prevent early tooth decay and subsequent loss. Some people actually brush their dog's teeth.

When your dog is an adult, his teeth might wear down with play. This is normal and not something to be overly concerned about, but have your veterinarian check on this from time-to-time. As the tooth wears down the nerve should recede, preventing the tooth from causing your dog any pain. Avoid using dirty or sandy discs. A dirty disc is tantamount to using revolving sandpaper on your dog's teeth every time he makes a catch. If you notice a chipped tooth or other tooth damage bring it to your veterinarian's attention immediately. Prompt attention may save a tooth.

You may notice that your dog seems to gulp his food without chewing. Since a dog's digestion does not begin in the mouth as it does with humans, it's only important that food passes down his throat to his stomach. (It is interesting to note that your dog does not need teeth to eat unless he hunts for his food.)

Nutrition

I feel that too many dog owners, doctors and veterinarians do not give enough thought to improper diet as the underlying cause of many

Mike Miller and Pro begin their routine with a sit command. This provides time to gather one's thoughts and settle down.

health problems for both people and dogs. Since you are responsible for your dog's health, you must select a nutritious and healthy brand.

Here are some items to keep in mind. A poor diet can seriously hurt your dog's health and shorten his life span. The best food for your dog is not necessarily the most expensive, as nutritional quality does not always go hand-in-hand with price.

I do not recommend feeding your dog table scraps. They are usually high in fat and will be as unhealthy for your dog's heart and circulatory system as they are for yours. Instead, look for a name-brand pet food, with the words *"complete and balanced,"* or *"provides 100% nutrition"* printed on the package. That way you'll ensure that your dog receives adequate nutrition. Finally, check with your veterinarian to see if your dog requires a normal diet, or a high protein diet because of the amount of exercise he gets.

Above all, do not overfeed your dog! A trim animal is a happy and healthy one. More pet owners doom their animals to disease and early deaths by overfeeding than from any other cause. There are no excuses for a fat dog! We may not be able to control what goes into our mouths, but we certainly can regulate what goes into theirs. Dogs still have some of their old instincts such as thinking they need to eat all they can whenever they can. They beg and look forlorn. Don't give in!

You should be able to run your hands over your dog's rib cage and feel his ribs but not see them. There also should be some definition between your dog's rib cage and his abdomen. Check with your veterinarian for more specifics.

I also do not recommend *free feeding*. This is where you leave

39

Always have water available for your dog.

food out so that your dog eats whenever he wants to. Whether your dog competes or just works out, it is better for him to be on a set schedule. Timed feedings allow you to monitor how much he eats which reflects how he feels and it also helps with housebreaking. I do recommend that you **always** leave water out for your dog. In the summer, make sure your dog's water is put in a cool or shady area because water left in the hot sun can easily become too hot to drink. In winter, water can freeze and be undrinkable.

While an occasional uncooked, solid (cooked bones can splinter) soup bone may be good for his teeth, avoid getting in the habit of rewarding your dog with *treats* for obedience. Your dog should perform because he loves you, loves what he does and appreciates your praise. Alex Stein, trainer of Ashley Whippet, calls this *"the enthusiasm factor." "The opportunity to catch the Frisbee disc is its own reward,"* he says.

Naming Your Dog

When you are ready to choose a name for your pet, give it some thought. Remember, your dog will have that name for the rest of his life. Once, when I was performing at a school, a teacher's aide approached me. While she petted Wizard, she told me how she loved dogs and had named one of her's *Stupid,* because as a pup it would sleep on the paper and wet on the floor. Her statement was staggering. Believe it or not, paper training is not genetic. Wild dogs do not intuitively look for paper to wet on.

My point is that you should seriously consider the name you give your dog, as it will psychologically affect how you and your friends relate to and view him. Also, remember that dogs are born *stupid* in the ways of man. It is up to us to educate them and if they fail, it is usually our fault. My dogs seem more like a Wizard and Magic every day. Your dog may seem more like an Aerial Annie, Bouncin' Boo, Hyper Hank, Leaping Luke or even a Casey, Dink, Gilbert, or Zach. But by naming your dog Stupid, it may be a self-fulfilling prophecy.

1986 World Champions Chris Barbo and Kato.

1989 World Champion, Gilbert about to make a lunging catch.

Grooming

Grooming is very important for your dog's health and appearance. The effort needed to groom your dog depends entirely on what breed you have. Therefore, I suggest that you ask your veterinarian for specifics.

I brush my dogs three times a week. I simultaneously examine their coat for ticks and fleas, their nails for length, their ears for dirt and mites and check their teeth for tartar buildup. Tartar can be seen as a hard, yellow coating on a dog's normally white teeth. It causes the gums to become red and inflamed and leads to gum disease that can in turn lead to the loss of healthy teeth. Although the use of dry food and dog biscuits can reduce the speed and amount of the buildup, a thorough cleaning including under the gums done by a veterinarian is recommended regularly.

I bathe my dogs when it looks like they need it, though normally not more than once a month, or so. Bathing too frequently can lead to dry skin. The warm weather may require weekly dips to control fleas as shampoos do not have any residual action against fleas.

Nails

Although nail care is a part of good grooming I wanted to highlight it here because if often gets neglected. Some people are under the mis-

Ken Pogson stylishly trims Richie's nails.

conception that a dog's nails will wear down enough by themselves through normal day-to-day activity. This is only **partially** true for a dog that works out a lot. Regardless, a dog's nails do not usually wear down evenly. Additionally, some dogs have dew-claws (thumb nails on front and/or back legs) that require special care. If you have a puppy you might consider having your veterinarian remove any dew-claws immediately. Wizard would even rip his trimmed dew claws because of his intensity in going for the disc.

Dogs that get less daily exercise definitely need nail care. Neglect in this area can cause your dog to hobble due to severe pain or may result in an injury to you in play. Don't subject your dog to this trauma, as you can easily trim his nails at home.

To trim your dog's nails you will need a dog nail clipper which is available at any pet store. If your dog has translucent nails, you can see the quick, the darker or pinkish area inside. Your dog's nails need clipping when they extend much beyond the quick. They should not, however, be cut **to** the quick. If you ask your veterinarian to show you how, I'm sure he or she will be happy to demonstrate the proper technique. If you cut into the quick by accident it will be painful to your dog and will cause bleeding. Control a small cut with a styptic pencil or a small amount of inert powder such as talcum or flour. If your dog's nails are all black you must exercise caution and concentrate only on the thinner tips.

Obedience

In the following Basic Training Techniques section I have outlined two methods that I feel have merit and are useful with

Your dog will usually go for the wettest, muddiest spot around to cool off. Nestle proudly demonstrates.

disc training. Whether you have trained a dog before or not, you should consider taking your dog to obedience school. This will help to socialize your dog early on before bad habits are formed. Instructors will also be able to point out areas you need work on. When working with their own dogs even experienced trainers can get into bad habits or overlook the obvious. I have experienced this first hand. Also, many good books are also available on the subject. I highly recommend the *Complete Book of Dog Training* and *Super-Training Your Dog* by Jo and Paul Loeb, both listed in the Appendix.

Dallas Dog and Disc club member Bethe Lehman enjoying a quiet moment with her dog Guthrie.

Each dog responds differently, but every trainer needs to include love, understanding, consistency and patience in a training regimen and in daily interaction with their dog.

It's only human to want your dog to be obedience trained and a Frisbee star overnight, but patience is the key to success. Keep initial workout sessions short, possibly as short as a few throws. It is better to have multiple short sessions per day than one long one. Stop **before** your dog gets tired so that he doesn't get the impression that Frisbee play or obedience is a chore. Work on one trick at a time or you may confuse your pet.

Once your dog has mastered a trick, start a new one while continuing to reinforce the old one. Each dog is different—some have fast stages of growth and development like human students while others progress more slowly. It's important to learn to recognize this and to train accordingly.

Begin your puppy's education as early as possible, starting when your pup is as young as three months old. Remember to always train in a fun, friendly and relaxed manner. At an early age your dog will have a very short attention span, so plan accordingly. Training should seem like a big game. Before your dog is three months old let him be a pup with few responsibilities.

I don't want to give the impression that you have to start with a puppy, but sometimes easier if you do. An adult dog, of any age and good health, can learn new tricks; it just takes a little longer because he may be a little more set or *corrupted* in his ways. For those older dogs not accustomed to strenuous physical activity, it is a good idea to encourage them to play at their own pace. When in doubt, consult your veterinarian!

Commands

Consistency is very important: always remember to use the same word for a particular command. I said *word* because it's important not to confuse your dog with long, drawn-out commands. It's easier for your dog to hear, differentiate and follow single-word commands. For example, say, "*Down,*" not "*Fluffy, please go lie down.*" Also, whatever you say, use an animated voice with a lot of inflection.

Four words that must become part of your dog's vocabulary are "*No, Down, Stay* and *Come.*" The reason I say this is because they can save your dog's life. For example "*No*" could be used to stop your dog from eating a sharp bone, while "*Down, Stay*" or "*Come*" might be used to prevent your dog from running into a busy street.

Sometimes the commands "*Down*" and "*Off*" get confused but they have completely different meanings and are important to differentiate. "*Down*" means lie down and "*Off*" means that your canine get off whatever he is on. Once, early in our marriage, my wife Lynn wanted Wizard to get off the couch and kept yelling, "*Down*" at him.

He continued to recline on the couch—looking somewhat puzzled as she repeated the command down. When I arrived, I told him, "*Off,*" and he immediately jumped from the sofa. Lynn just glared at me. Once you have come up with various commands, make sure that others in contact with your dog know what they are.

One last word of advice. Be careful in choosing your release word. A release word is one that you use to tell your dog to relax. For instance, when you tell your

Three-time World Champion Bouncin' Boo.

dog to stay, you also need a command to tell him that he can now do as he pleases. You also might use a release word to tell your dog that he can get out of the car or cross the street. Some books recommend the word "*Okay*," but since this word is used so often in daily communication, a dog can be released unintentionally. There are two options for choosing a release word. The first is to choose a word that you would rarely use in normal con-

versation. The second is to make up a word that would never come up in conversation. I use a made up word, "*Kea*," pronounced "*Key-ah*."

The Gary Larson cartoon, shown above, illustrates what your dog hears and what he understands. In most cases, dogs do not speak or understand our language naturally, so keep it simple for them.

Crate Training

I won't go into this in detail as most dog books cover this method. However, I highly recommend the concept of crate training. Basically, a crate or kennel is, a plastic carrier or shipping container made especially for animals. It will prevent your dog from unattended chewing of your favorite items, is a good way to teach housebreaking, makes for a safe retreat and finally is a secure way to travel with your pet. The correct size of crate will allow your dog to stand up and turn around comfortably. I recommend getting a crate which your dog will grow into rather than out of as they can be used throughout your dog's life.

When Alex Stein had several Whippets, he would stack all their kennels in a row (three high) and call them "*doggie condos.*" They loved it.

Basic Training Techniques

For most of Wizard and Magic's training I used a common technique I call guiding. For example, with the sit command, I would gently push their hindquarters to the floor until they sat, while saying, "*Sit.*" I then kept them in the sitting position and praised them for being so smart. This is very important. I praised them although the whole process was controlled by me. Any time you give your dog love and attention he will try to please you to receive more of the same. He will work at figuring out what pleases you and will continue to do it.

I can't stress enough the importance of rewarding your dog both verbally (by praising him) and physically (by petting him). I am not a strong believer in using food treats to train animals. At times during initial training you might consider a food treat, but generally it is not necessary. In fact, used incorrectly, treats can be detrimental to a dog's performance and become a crutch. Your dog can get to the point where he will refuse to work without a treat. The proper way is to get him to **want** to perform and play because he enjoys it and because it pleases you so much.

Praise your dog from the time he begins to get the idea until the time he masters the trick, and before you know it, he will be doing it correctly. Wizard and Magic can catch easily, but I still acknowledge their accomplishments verbally and physically to let them know I am pleased. Dogs thrive on love, attention and recognition. I have never given Wizard a food treat of any kind for doing a trick. I just pet him and say words like, "*Good boy, way to go, Wiz.*" Plenty of praise and the fun of the game will keep your dog very happy and playing in top form. On the other hand, I have used food treats with Magic on several occasions. Wizard and Magic are as different as night and day and it is important to recognize that no two canines can be trained exactly alike.

An alternative is the patience method, where you wait until your dog does what you want without pulling, pushing or coaching. Using the same exam-

Peter Bloeme guiding Wizard into a sit.

JACKIE BERNARD

ple as above, I would wait until Wizard sat, then say, "*Sit*" a few times and congratulate him for desired behavior.

I have used this method successfully many times. It was good for house-breaking. I would take Wizard and Magic outside and when they relieved themselves I would say, "*Out.*" I kept doing this until I could say, "*Out*" and they knew it was time to eliminate. This skill is more valuable than it may seem at first. For example, before competition or a demonstration I would walk my dog and say, "*Out*" so that he wouldn't have to stop in the middle of his routine for a nature break. This prevented both embarrassment to me and an interruption in our performance.

Jurassic Frisbee.

Another way this method can be used is with the command "*Speak.*" Just wait until your dog's favorite someone (possibly the mailman) shows up at your door. When your dog starts to bark, say, "*Speak.*" After doing this a few times he will have learned to speak on command (or look for the mailman).

Another example of the patience method is apparent in the way I taught Wizard and Magic the back flip. The back flip is a trick that is repeatable and predictable, yet I couldn't easily guide them through it. I would have them jump backwards with an intentionally crooked throw and when they went for the catch, I'd say, "*Back.*" After a while they got the idea that when I said back, they should make a back flip to catch the throw.

Every so often it is a good idea to test your dog and put him on notice that you will not always be using the same order in your commands. In demonstrations I would tell Wizard to sit, then lie down, then roll-over at the beginning of our routine. It got so familiar to Wizard that when we were in a show situation and I said, "*Sit*" at the beginning of the show he would sit, lie down and roll-over in one continuous motion. Dogs can be **too** smart at times. Keep your dog honest: mix up the order on occasion. The next time I said, "*Down, Sit, Down, Roll.*" He was so embarrassed when he did it wrong that he started to listen again.

Melissa Heeter and Radical Rush.

Common Injuries

Most of the time, when you use common sense, playing with a disc with your dog is safe. Still, there are two things that commonly occur that you should be aware of. A sharp edge on a disc can cut a dog's lip, tongue or gums during play. Even when your disc is new at the beginning of your session, it can become sharp during play.

Also, your dog will occasionally bite his tongue. This is not surprising since **people** often bite their tongues when eating, and your dog is using his mouth to catch a moving disc! This will more likely occur after your dog is hot and panting. Since a dog's tongue is used for cooling purposes it tends to hang out when the animal is hot. When your panting canine starts to chomp down on a disc without fulling reeling in his tongue, bleeding is the inevitable result. Some cold water should stop the bleeding quickly. Consult with your veterinarian if you are concerned about excessive bleeding.

The two worst causes of injuries are not Frisbee-related; they are car accidents and dog fights. Both can almost always be prevented with common sense, proper obedience training and the use of a leash.

Discipline

Never hit your dog! If your dog does not obey you, it is probably your fault for not teaching him properly. I realize that training can be occasionally frustrating, but it is both dangerous to your dog's health and unproductive to his cooperation and understanding if you use violence. I'm sure the same could be said about children. You want a dog to respect you, not fear you. If you must punish your dog, there are various, safe methods such as using a stern vocal tone and level. This form of punishment usually works well. At the extreme, if your dog commits a serious offense, such as something that may endanger his life, you may have to resort to grabbing the back of your dog's neck, shaking and scolding him. This is sometimes known as a *scruff shake*. This is apparently very similar to what a mother dog would do to scold a pup. It looks a lot worse to bystanders than it is, but it gets a dog's attention.

World Finalists Mark Wood and Zach.

Disc Basics

ne of the most important things in training your dog for disc play is, surprisingly enough, for **you** to throw adequately and accurately. Remember, you are a member of a team and it isn't fair to let your partner down. Developing your throwing skills will enhance your dog's catching potential. I have often seen dogs with great abilities score poorly in competition due to their owner's consistently bad throws. Even Wizard has looked less than a champ because of throwing errors made by friends and celebrities (sometimes even by me). I recommend that you learn to throw before playing with a Frisbee disc with your dog so you won't confuse him or give him bad catching habits.

Disc Selection

There are many differences in flying discs and because of their various colors, shapes, sizes and materials, some are obviously more suited to canine play than others. Most discs are made out of cloth, rubber and most commonly plastic. As a collector with over 3,000 different flying discs and as an owner of a disc patent, I have seen just about every disc imaginable.

The Fastback Frisbee disc by Wham-O Manufacturing Company offers the best overall characteristics for play with adult dogs. It is currently the official disc of the Friskies Canine Frisbee Championships. It weighs in at approximately 106 grams (about four ounces) and is 9.25" in diameter. The

Original Fastback Frisbee.

Fastback model was originally designed as a sleek sports model but when sales weren't as expected due to its poor flight performance, Wham-O redesigned it and turned it into a premium disc (used in advertising). As canine disc play increased in popularity, enthusiasts gravitated to it because of its size, weight, material (made out of a soft polyethelyne plastic), and sloping edge (which makes it easier for your dog to catch). In addition, its flight plate contains ridges which provide a good griping surface even when coated with doggie slobber.

A new disc that shows a lot of promise for canine play is the 9.25", 104 gram Zephyr from Innova-Champion Discs, Inc., a company of disc champions and enthusiasts. The company began primarily as a manufacturer of discs for the popular sport of disc golf (similar to ball golf) and now is branching out into other disc sports.

While Wham-O's Frisbee discs have concentric rings or ridges on them that promote a good grip, this new disc from Innova has a unique feature called a thumb track, a ridge that encourages proper placement of your thumb. When I first picked up the Zephyr my thumb fell in the ridge and my grip felt solid. A solid grip is the first step in being able to throw a disc. Also, because the disc was originally developed for disc golf, it is more aerodynamically sound than your average dog disc.

Flying Dog Products carries both the Wham-O Fastback and the Innova Zephyr along with other Frisbee dog-related materials in its mail order catalog. *(See Appendix for more information.)*

Whichever disc you choose, remember that your dog will be catching it in his mouth with his **teeth.** Puppies have sharp but fragile needle-like teeth. Obviously, it is not a good idea to get the standard

The Zephyr disc from Innova.

monster-sized disc out to play with your pup. You want his adult teeth to safely grow in naturally with proper development and strength. I started Wizard with a Mini-Frisbee disc, which is three inches in diameter, because I didn't want to knock his teeth out. Then we moved up to a very soft, 5-inch diameter disc and finally to the common, nine-inch size when he was 6 months old. I don't recommend using the large model, except as a food dish and for basic training until his adult teeth grow in.

Dogs are colorblind, so the color of your disc is important mainly for creating contrasting images. To a dog, some background colors will look the same as the Frisbee disc you are using, so make it easy on him by

Dog with a hard mouth.

PHIL VAN TEE

using one that will stand out from its surroundings. For example, blue and red would be my favorite choices for use in an open area on a overcast day. A light-colored disc should stand out well against a blue sky. At dusk, when colors are fading, humans start to have trouble seeing (without lights), but dogs can still see well. The color used in competition is usually white as we always hope our events will be held on blue sky, sunny days.

Speaking of sight, keep in mind that because of his head height, your dog has a different perspective on everything than you do. He most often focuses on objects at his eye level and therefore has to look up to see the same object that you or I can see straight ahead. This may help you understand why your dog will or will not do certain things. Keep this in mind during training. For example, the reason your dog may not jump over something is that he can't see what awaits him on the other side. So, at first, position your dog so that he has a full view of his surroundings.

Dogs have better peripheral vision than we do—up to 120 degrees. This means that they will be more adept at spotting and catching throws off to the side than you might think possible. This capability is invaluable in disc sports.

Gimmicks

There are many flying disc *gimmicks* on the market; some are even specifically geared toward dog owners. They may be great for adult play and collecting, but generally I recommend that you stick with reliable, safe discs for your dog.

One gimmick disc I have seen advertised in catalogs catering to the dog owner is the Whistle Disc. This disc whistles as it flies, making it fun for people but not for dogs. Three evenly spaced whistles are built into the rim, just where your dog catches it. If your dog grabs a Whistle Disc in the air, his mouth or tongue could easily be cut by the whistles in the edge. If you must buy it, keep it as a collectable and do not use it around pets or children.

The Whistle Disc.

I also don't recommend the Aerobie for general canine play. This disc is a highly designed flying ring that is quite expensive. Lately, there has been much talk about how easy this product is to throw and how far it flies. In fact, I was asked to write a book about it but declined. While there is no question that it flies far and is easy to throw, for normal play with your dog it has too narrow a profile and flies too fast. However, for use as a prop as Jendi Holmes is shown doing in the photo below, it can be an interesting variation in exhibitions.

Finally, *scented* discs have been introduced for dogs by Wham-O and other disc manufacturers. Although this is an interesting variation on air pollution, you may wonder why anyone would make a scented disc. Apparently the research and development *wizards* at these companies decided that if a disc were made that smelled like food, you would be more likely to buy it, thinking your dog would love you for it. On the contrary, it will probably drive you both crazy. Besides, you don't want him to eat the thing, just catch it. Again I recommend that you use a *plain,* unscented disc.

World Finalist Jendi Holmes and Scotland demonstrating short throws with an Aerobie.

Other Discs

There are a few other disc products that you may come in contact with in pet stores. The first is a premium disc. These usually feature the store's name and are generally poor knockoffs of the Fast-back Frisbee disc. They can be made out of stiff plastic, have a sharp edge and be incorrectly shaped for proper flight. There are a few different brands of these discs but I don't recommend them.

You may also see discs with bone shaped tops. The bone shape on the flight plate hurts its aerodynamic flight and adds unnecessary weight. The bone top disc was originally designed to help dogs in picking it up from the ground. However, since any serious Frisbee dog will be required to pick up their misses or your poor throws with plain, flat-topped discs, you may as well practice with the real thing instead of a gimmick.

World Finalist Rhett Butler.

Then there are some discs that are made out of a very inflexible material. Although highly durable, they are much too hard and rigid for canine play and hold a high potential for mouth and tooth injuries. I see no use at all for the rigid model.

There are also some discs sold that are made out out of a material which is very soft and highly resistant to doggie bites. Unfortunately, they are so soft and pliable that they tend to fold up upon release and thus are difficult to throw. Still, the small version of this disc (about 3" in diameter) is good for starting out with your puppy as it is a bit sturdier.

By the way, for those dog owners who include warm weather swimming as part of their dog's training, it is important to note that many of these special discs will **not** float. Make sure that you test your favorite disc in shallow water first to protect your investment.

Finally, it is interesting to note that some discs even come with a booklet detailing various training methods that look, not surprisingly, like the Ashley Whippet Invitational's copyrighted training booklet.

Fabric Training Discs

My dogs have *soft mouths* which means they try to cradle the disc when making a catch thereby not doing much damage to it. On the other hand, some dogs like Jeff Perry's canine Gilbert, the 1989 World

Small dogs enjoy the sport of canine Frisbee as much as larger ones.

Getting your dog to release the disc is sometimes easier said than done.

1989 World Champion Gilbert shows good form and muddy paws in this artistic Japanese photo with Mt. Fuji in the background.

Champion, has as hard a mouth as they come. He bites through and tries to *pulverize* the disc on every toss. Perry writes:

*"Professional bird dog train-
ers go to great lengths to ensure
that their dogs have 'soft mouths'
(a dog with a soft mouth retrieves
birds without further damage).
Some trainers use dummy birds
wrapped in barbed wire to reinforce the idea in the minds of
young 'trainees' that birds are to*

Soft Bite Floppy Disc.

*be handled with care. Unfortunately, there is very little that a Frisbee
dog owner can do to train his dog to catch with a soft mouth.*

*"Although some dogs snare discs gently, most of them seem to
take great pleasure in reducing a flying disc to its chemical components as quickly as possible. For these dogs, there are fabric discs now
available in pet stores.*

*"The fabric discs are safe, durable and good for starting out pups
as there can be no fear of being hit or breaking something indoors.*

*"As test subjects I used my dog Gilbert, a short-haired Pointer who
weighs approximately 50 pounds and Annie Oakley, a mixed female
weighing about 35 pounds. Gilbert has the proven capability to reduce
a Fastback Frisbee disc to fragments in minutes. Over the past nine
years, his nimble teeth have shortened the life spans of several hundred
discs. Annie while not as destructive, is try-
ing hard to follow in Gilbert's pawsteps.*

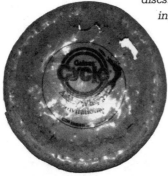

*"I began the test by engaging in
a typical practice session lasting
approximately 30 minutes. It consisted of short and long throws at
various angles and spins, also an
assortment of standard tricks. After
practice I carefully examined the fabric discs. Remarkably, they showed
virtually no damage or wear. For
general fetching and catching purposes, the fabric disc proved highly
resistant to damage.*

Fastback disc after a few minutes
with Gilbert. Doggie owner's idea of
a nightmare.

"I also found an additional, perhaps less obvious benefit of the fabric discs. Their relative flexibility and softness could reduce the likelihood of mouth injuries caused by sharp protruding shards of plastic sometimes present on worn Frisbee discs.

"One difficulty that I have with the fabric disc is that it simply doesn't seem to be as pleasing for a dog to catch as a regular plastic disc. The usual solid chomp is replaced by a non-event...silence. Gilbert's and Annie's catches of the fabric disc seemed almost timid in comparison with their aggressive grabs of standard plastic discs. Still, timidity not-withstanding, they did catch the fabric disc as consistently as the standard Frisbee disc.

"From the thrower's perspective, the fabric disc takes a little getting used to. The disc that I tested was approximately the same size and weight as a standard Fastback Frisbee disc. When held, the fabric disc feels flimsy. Because of the non-rigidity of the material, it is difficult to impart much spin on the disc and thus long-distance throws are difficult. Also, many throws are a bit more wobbly than throws with a more rigid disc, but practice with the fabric disc can smooth out your flights.

"For those dog owners who use the disc in a non-aerodynamic manner (e.g., end-over-end, inverted, etc.) the fabric disc is somewhat difficult to throw because of its flexibility. Rapid wrist snaps cause it to deform and absorb energy rather than spinning or flipping end-over-end as rapidly as a standard disc would when thrown in an identical manner.

"In conclusion, I feel that it is highly unlikely that the fabric disc will replace the standard Wham-O Fastback Frisbee disc as the disc of choice for the sport of canine

ROBERT OZANKAN

It appears as if 1991 World Champion Maggy is trying out for a new Come 'N Get It bag.

Frisbee. Still, as a general purpose training disc, the fabric disc definitely fills a void and could save a Frisbee dog enthusiast much money over a dog's career."

Disc Maintenance

Frisbee discs generally don't require much care and maintenance, but here are a few tips to improve your game. During practice you should

"Really dad, I don't think this one is dirty."

use a towel to keep the disc clean and dry. Eliminating the *slime factor* will help keep your throws consistent.

You'll probably notice that with play, your discs will develop rough and sharp edges. If you leave them that way they can cut your dog's mouth. The remedy is simple: use fine grade sandpaper to smooth the edges after every couple of play sessions. Between practice sessions, I recommend that you wash off the discs so there is no dirt, saliva or sandpaper grit left on them, making them more sanitary and safer for your dog. This can be done by hand or in the dishwasher.

Of course there are some dogs who insist on putting their teeth through the disc on every throw. For these dog owners there is very little maintenance necessary. After each day of practice they simply throw the discs away. I haven't known anyone who could alter their dog's bite from hard to soft during disc training, so don't encourage it. This is one reason I don't believe in a lot of tug-of-war with a disc. Don't give your dog bad habits you will later regret.

How do dogs fly?

PHIL VAN TEE

Flying Disc Aerodynamics

The edge of a flying Frisbee disc operates under the same scientific principles as an airfoil, mean-

61

Two-time World Champions Jeff Gabel and Casey.

ing it is designed to produce reaction from the air. The concept is simple. The air that passes over the disc travels faster than the air passing underneath, which causes a low pressure area above. The air underneath is not affected by the airfoil, so it moves up to fill this void, causing the disc to rise.

Since a flying disc spins like a gyroscope, additional properties come into play. The disc not only needs forward motion but also spin for its stability. One or the other is not enough. Just try pushing the disc through the air with no spin. You'll find that it flutters and falls.

A flying disc cannot accelerate once it has been thrown, so your initial release is critical.

Another consideration is the angle of release. Is the leading edge of the disc pointed up or down? Too far up and the disc will come back to you. Too far down and it will dive to the ground. What about the side position? Is it angled up or down? If it's too extreme one way or the other, it will either slice or hook. You can experiment with the following elements after you master the basic throws: skips, curves, floaters and distance flights.

When outside forces such as wind and weather conditions come into play, you can see why just one type of throw can fly so many different ways. Weather cannot be controlled, but you can work with it and take advantage of it. Weather is an element that even the most experienced competitors often overlook.

Smooth-coated Fox Terrier Sparky.

Ginger jumping for joy during the taping of a Japanese television commercial for Friskies.

Throwing

The framework for all throws is similar and includes grip, spin, stance and general elements. Practice the different grips and throws at short distances. As you develop control, gradually increase your distance.

General Elements

The most important rule to remember when starting out is to keep the Frisbee disc's flight as flat as possible. The disc will react differently if released angled nose down or up or angled to one side or the other.

It is rare that you will find perfect weather conditions (no wind) for practice, unless you have access to an indoor site such as the Pontiac Silverdome. Therefore, always try to throw long throws across the wind, not downwind or into the wind. Once you are proficient as a thrower you may choose to throw into the wind for extra float time. When you do this you take the risk of the disc moving up or down suddenly just as your dog jumps for it. Throwing downwind will make your throws go further with little effort. However, downwind throws provide the least control, requiring your dog to run faster and guarantee minimal float time for your dog to catch up to the disc.

During Mini-Distance, throw into the wind for great-

LONG PHOTOGRAPHY, INC.

World Finalist Stan Sellers launches Zulu.

World Finalist Brian Lamky making a backhand throw to Tatiana in Mini-Distance.

est control and float time. However, when throwing into the wind you will need to release the disc with lots of spin and with a steep angle (almost perpendicular to the ground with the edge of the disc towards the ground), not flat. Think of having to cut through the wind. The disc will normally turn in the direction that it is spinning. For example, for a righthanded thrower making a backhand throw, the disc will turn to the right with the clockwise spin that it's released with.

At first, practice only short-range throws (10 to 15 feet) that are released between waist and shoulder height. **Gradually** increase the distance of your throws as you succeed at shorter distances. Attempting to increase distance before mastering the basics can cause many technical and mechanical problems due to overexertion. You want to make smooth, level and accurate throws and build upon success.

A good way to practice your throws is against a baseball backstop. Mark a spot with tape or ribbon on the backstop. Take a supply of ten discs and step back about ten feet. Try to hit the mark with good flat, spinning throws. As your accuracy improves move back five feet at a time.

Grip

Use a firm but not tight grip to hold the Frisbee disc. Make sure that the disc is firmly in your palm and that you aren't holding it just with your fingers. After you develop a comfortable grip, practice it repeatedly until it becomes second nature. As in golf and tennis, a good grip is paramount to success.

Spin

Always put a good amount of spin on the disc upon release. The more spin, the longer the disc will hold its stability. At first, beginners can simply concentrate on wrist snap. Ideally, however, spin is imparted to a disc through several factors, including proper body position and a snapping motion that originates from a steady stance and progresses through the hips, arm, elbow and finally, the wrist. At first think of snapping your arm (gently) like a whip rather than using a full follow through. It is similar to using a rolled up towel and snapping it.

Stance

For a proper stance, your feet should be a shoulders' width apart with your knees slightly bent and parallel to each other. Your forward shoulder should point toward your target. For most standing throws except the sidearm, start with two-thirds of your weight on your back foot. Then shift it naturally forward to your front foot (leaving one-third of your weight on your back foot) upon release and delivery. Don't lift your back foot off the ground and lunge forward; always keep some weight on each foot. For the sidearm throw, you will start with two-thirds of your weight on your back foot as with the other throws but do not shift your weight forward upon release.

Throws (as described for right handed throwers)

There are many different grips and deliveries. The ones that I explain here will give you a solid foundation of Frisbee basics to practice before you begin training your dog.

Backhand

The backhand throw is a versatile and easy to learn delivery. Once mastered, it can be used for accuracy, distance and trick throws.

I recommend a combination of popular grips called *the modified Berkeley power grip*. Make a fist with your palm up; open your thumb to the *hitchhiking* position. Loosen your fingers just enough to slip the disc between your palm and finger tips and place your thumb down on top. This will probably feel awkward. It is called the Berkeley power grip—best for pure distance, but difficult to control. Now, bring your other hand up and hold the other side of the disc tem-

Backhand Delivery (front): full motion from beginning to release.

Backhand Delivery (side): full motion from beginning to release.

The disc should be released at the angle shown above left if into the wind or flat as shown center if there is little wind. The angle shown above right is incorrect.

A Study in Contrasts: *Both competitors are using the backhand delivery in Mini-Distance. Top: World Finalist Paul Gebauer using incorrect throwing form. Gebauer appears to be holding his breath, pulling his rear arm backward and coming off his rear foot. Above: 1993 World Champion Gary Suzuki using correct throwing form. Suzuki is exhaling upon delivery, keeping his rear arm in a neutral position and keeping both feet firmly planted. The importance of Mini-Distance cannot be over stated. (I have flipped the photos of Suzuki to make him appear right handed for comparison purposes.)*

69

Backhand Grip: side, top and bottom (modified Berkeley Power Grip).

porarily. Move the fingers of your gripping hand slightly toward your thumb (while trying to maintain as much contact as possible with the inside/bottom rim) until they feel somewhat comfortable. **Do not** go so far as to place your index finger along the outside edge of the disc, since doing so would cause you to lose accuracy and control. Now you have the modified grip. Make sure the grip pressure is not between your thumb and first two fingers but the last two fingers and your palm. This will allow you to snap the throw. It may seem like a subtle change but it can really affect your throwing.

If you are right handed, stand with your right foot forward. Bring the disc back across your body to just above your left side until your arm is as far back as your left shoulder. Your arm should be bent slightly, with your wrist bent inward and the disc held flat.

The throwing motion should be left to right, smooth and even, with a good snap upon release. Do not rotate your wrist from side to side, only forward and backward as if you were doing wrist curls with a dumbbell. Follow through with your right hand (not just the finger) pointing at your target. Keep your eyes forward. If your throw goes to the left of the target you've released it too soon, to the right, too late. Most people fall into the too-late category and hook their throw to the right. Usually the disc will end up where ever your first finger ends up pointing.

If the disc wobbles, check your grip, speed up your delivery and concentrate on keeping the disc level from your release to your dog's catch.

Roller

The roller throw is commonly used in training a Frisbee dog. It allows them to easily see and track (follow) a moving disc as it stays on the same level throughout.

For this throw, use the backhand grip. The throwing angle is steep, almost vertical. Bring your arm toward your chest and snap

Roller Delivery (front): full motion from beginning to release.

Roller Delivery (side): full motion from beginning to release.

your wrist forward and down. Make sure to bend down or kneel close to the ground so that your throw will roll, not bounce. Your release should be perpendicular to the ground. Roller throws are great for introducing puppies or new trainees to the motion of the disc as they are especially easy for canines to see, track and follow.

Upside-Down Slider

This is also an excellent throw for a puppy and is also best thrown from a kneeling position. Grip the disc as shown on page 72. Basically, the upside-down grip is the opposite or mirror image of the backhand grip. From the modified Berkeley power grip you replace the disc you are holding with a disc that is upside-down. You may have to move your fingers slightly to get comfortable. This time your grip pressure should be between your thumb which is against the rim, and your first finger. Instead of releasing the disc in the air, throw it flat and close to the ground so that it skims across the ground like a hockey puck. This throw can be used indoors with great success.

Upside-Down Grip Views: side, top and bottom.

Upside-Down Slider Delivery (side): full motion from beginning to release.

Upside-Down

The upside-down throw is great for variety (for you and your dog) and can be made from a standing or kneeling position. It's also challenging and unusual. Since the disc is upside-down, it doesn't float in the air as right side up throws do, it **falls.** As it is the easiest to do, I will describe the backhand version of the upside-down throw.

Use the same stance as the backhand throw but use the upside-down grip as shown previously. Instead of bringing your arm across your body in a parallel motion as you did with the backhand throw, start the disc at shoulder level and snap the throw out. Release the disc slightly above head level. Make your throw a little higher so it will flatten out as it falls to your partner or dog. This can be done standing or kneeling. You will need to adjust your release angle depending on wind and distance.

Upside-down Delivery (front): full motion from beginning to release.

Upside-down Delivery (side): full motion from beginning to release.

Advanced Throws

Since the level of competition has grown tremendously over the past few years, I feel that it is important to mention a few advanced throws that are now commonly used in canine disc play.

Sidearm

The sidearm is an advanced, but common throw in which only three fingers are used to grip the disc. Turn the disc upside-down. Make a *peace* or *victory* sign with your first two fingers. Place your middle finger against the inside rim while keeping your first finger flat against the flight plate (the bottom of the disc, not the rim). Grip the top with your thumb. Turn the disc right-side-up. Your last two fingers are

73

bent and used as a guide. Your grip pressure should be between your thumb and palm not your fingers. This time, stand with your left foot and shoulder toward your partner. The arm motion will be from right

Sidearm Grip Views: side, top and bottom.

Sidearm Delivery (front): full motion from beginning to release.

Sidearm Delivery (side): full motion from beginning to release.

to left. Bend your arm in a 90 degree angle and keep your elbow close to your body. Bend your wrist back and then snap it forward. Concentrate on using mostly wrist action rather than arm motion for this throw. The angle of the disc upon release should be at approximately five o'clock. This one may take a bit of practice. Usually your thumb ends up pointing in the general direction of the flight path of the disc.

The best use of the basic sidearm throw I've seen is by 1991 World Champion Ron Ellis with his dog Maggy. He has a four-throw combination where he throws short, 10-yard tosses back and forth to her. He alternates between backhand and sidearm deliveries. One throw is a soft floater that she must leap up to catch. She then races back in the opposite direction and grabs a soft backhand.

Jeff Gabel, a two-time world champion, used an advanced version of the sidearm throw with great success. He would run toward his dog Casey, who would also run toward him. As his dog got close to him, Gabel would leap over his dog and throw a between-the-legs sidearm in the direction the dog was going. Casey seemed to kick in the afterburners and take off after it to make the catch.

Overhand Wristflip

The overhand wristflip grip is the same as the upside-down grip shown earlier including the amount and placement of grip pressure. Like the sidearm throw, stand with your left foot and shoulder toward your partner. The arm motion will be from right to left. Your throwing arm should almost be straight with the disc almost resting on top of the arm. This throw is similar to the sidearm in that you don't use a lot of body motion. Release the Frisbee at three to four o'clock. Like the backhand throw, this throw will usually go where your index finger ends up pointing.

Overhand Wristflip Grip: side, top and bottom.

Overhand Wristflip Delivery (side): full motion from beginning to release.

Overhand Wristflip Delivery (front): full motion from beginning to release.

Butterfly

Frisbee discs are most commonly thrown vertically, horizontally, or upside down. Although the disc flies best these ways, they are not the only options. Popular with the dogs is the butterfly (also known as end-over-end or third-world spin) where the disc flips or tumbles to the dog. Again, there are many variations of this throw and variations in the use of it.

Here is the basic throw which you can expand on later: Hold the disc with your left hand at eye level. Reach under the disc with your right hand to the leading edge so that your four fingers are facing you on top and your thumb is on the bottom. This is the only throw where the disc should not be resting deeply in your palm but approximately where your fingers join your hand. Let go of the disc with your left hand so that you have a grip with the right. This is the basic grip. To throw the disc snap down and forward. The disc

Butterfly Grip: bottom and top.

should go about three or four feet and be flipping end-over-end. *(See page 104, to understand how your dog will catch this one.)*

Butterfly Delivery (front): full motion from beginning to release.

Butterfly Delivery (side): full motion from beginning to release.

Two-Handed

This is an excellent all-round throw for variety and short distances; it gives you tremendous control of the Frisbee disc's angle.

Explaining this throw in words is more difficult than the throw itself (see photos below). I hope you will be able to use the text and photos to learn it. Open your hands flat and put them together so they are touching in a prayer-type position, with fingers pointed up at eye level. Move them apart wide enough to insert the disc so that it rests even with the center point of your middle fingers. Without letting go of the disc, rotate it in a clockwise direction until the back of your right hand is in front of your nose. The disc should still be level. If this is done correctly there should be a little tension. You might even rest the disc slightly on the outside of your left thumb at this point.

To make the throw, push with your right hand and pull with your

Two-Handed Grip: side, top and bottom.

Two-handed Delivery (front): full motion from beginning to release.

left, moving the disc in a counter-clockwise motion to give it spin. Simultaneously use your arms to direct the throw above your head.

This throw also can be made in a forward motion by starting with the disc over your head and spinning and pushing the disc forward.

Skip

A skip occurs when the disc *bounces* off the ground and back into the air. I don't consider it very useful for Frisbee dogs because it is very difficult to do on grass. Still, some people do use the skip in competition for variety. It is difficult for a beginner to learn a skip throw on grass, so practice it on a hard surface first. (Remember, never play with your dog on concrete, asphalt or other hard surfaces for obvious safety reasons.)

Use the backhand grip, but instead of holding and throwing the disc at a level attitude, you throw it with an extreme angle, about seven o'clock, almost perpendicular to the ground. Most people think that you try to hit the leading or front edge of the disc but it is actually the side edge that hits. This throw needs a lot of spin and good forward motion. Think of it as a hard curve that hits the ground. This will take some experimentation. Once you have mastered this throw on a hard surface, practice it on short grass where you must throw it harder to get the same effect.

1980 competitor and dog at the Rose Bowl in Pasadena.

Tapping/Tipping

Technically, tapping belongs in the basics section because it can be combined with the two-handed throw. But it is also an advanced trick. Originally developed in human competition as a unique move for the *freestyle* event, it was used to impress the audience and fellow competitors. Hit the bottom of the disc with your finger as it floats to you during its descent and then make the catch. This can be combined with a two-handed throw over your head and tapped to your dog who makes the catch. For variation, you can do this with different parts of your body. Try tapping the disc with your elbow, knee or foot.

Greater Atlanta Dog and Disc members Dave Huffine and Sparky.

Basic Training

n general, until your dog is two to three months old just let him be a puppy without a care in the world. In fact, you may want to wait until that age before getting a dog, since he may need the time with his mother and siblings for proper development.

At three months you may begin teaching basic tricks, including disc basics. At six months you can begin training in earnest without overemphasizing jumping. And, at one year you should have a firm foundation so that you and your dog can work on advanced techniques.

Long Line Leash Training

Many times in your training it will be helpful to train your dog on a long leash sometimes called a long line. This is an item that is easily made with a laundry cord and dog clip as shown below. A cord of about 30 feet is a good all-around size. On one end add a loop for your hand, on the other securely tie a dog clip which you attach to your dog's collar. Be especially careful of two things when using this long line. First, make sure that your dog doesn't get tangled up in it. Don't begin training until the rope is free of knots and tangles. Second, be especially aware of rope burn. If your canine runs past you and the rope should drag against your exposed skin, expect a nasty surprise.

A long line is commonly used to develop long-range verbal control. Controlling your dog not only ensures good performances, it also may prevent unfortunate confrontations with people, cars and other dogs.

Home made long line training leash.

Make sure that you train him not only to get along with strangers, but to be sociable with other dogs that might be in the area. Begin socializing your dog as a puppy by getting him around lots of people (adults and children) and dogs at fairs, parks and puppy training classes. An obedient dog is a happy and safe dog. Any signs of aggressive behavior should be taken seriously and properly dealt with.

Workout Area

At first, and later for variety, you can hold training sessions inside your home. There are usually fewer distractions indoors than there are outside. Still, after working a short time indoors, your dog will point out all the distractions there are in the room, down to the dust on the floor.

Once you move outside, you shouldn't play on hard dirt, asphalt, concrete, near automobiles or broken glass. Both asphalt and concrete become extremely hot in the summer and cold in the winter. Many people don't realize this but running on these surfaces, even when cool, will tear and damage the pads on a dog's feet. This is even true of surfaces similar to clay courts in tennis. The danger of cars speaks for itself.

For real workouts, you will need to go outside to a grassy area that is somewhat level and free of obstacles. A fenced-in back yard is ideal. Always make sure that your dog has a collar with your name, address and telephone number in case he gets spooked and runs away.

Whether it is the law in your area or not, clean up after your dog so that you and other dog owners will always be welcome in the park. Be aware of local ordinances that require your dog to be on-leash in certain areas.

A safe workout area is important for everyone!

PHIL VAN TEE

One of the best (and safest) workout methods for strengthening and conditioning your dog is with warm weather water training. Once your dog has learned to swim, throw his favorite toy (preferably a disc but make sure it floats first), into the water so that he has to swim out and bring it back. Repeat this until you feel that he has had a good

Morgan demonstrates the fun of water training.

workout. Water training is the perfect way to provide low-impact aerobic conditioning without jarring your dog's joints. Do this occasionally to supplement land sessions. Don't forget to remove your dog's flea collar before he swims. The flea-killing chemicals used in most collars are intensified by water and can pose a threat to your dog's health in high doses.

A perfect example of using the water for strengthening and conditioning was when 1991 World Champion Ron Ellis' dog Maggy sustained a non-Frisbee related injury to one of her legs seven weeks before a Regional competition. Ron allowed her to rest completely for four weeks. At that point, he doubted that she would be ready for the rigors of the tough competition, so with his veterinarian's advice he decided to start Maggy swimming simply for therapy and exercise. Fellow competitors Bob and Marilyn Evans generously offered the use of their backyard pool every day during the week before the competition. Maggy's condition improved dramatically. Although Ellis and Maggy could only practice four times in seven weeks, Maggy won the Regional title!

Many experts recommend against having your dog swim in a chlorinated pool or in saltwater because dogs can get sick by drinking the water. Therefore, train your dog to not drink bath, pool or lake water. Always provide your dog with fresh drinking water. Rivers and lakes are great for training but beware of local hazards such as underwater obstacles, and in some places even alligators.

Weather Conditions

Pay attention to temperature and humidity when you are working out. Remember, your dog has a fur coat. Whether your dog has short or long hair, it's easy for him to get overheated in warm weather because he cannot sweat (as humans do) to dissipate heat. Panting is the dog's primary method of internal cooling. Never leave your dog locked in a car even with the windows open. On a hot day an automo-

Three-time World Champion Bouncin' Boo taking a water break.

bile can quickly turn into an oven. A dog's normal body temperature is 101.5 degrees and in the summertime even a short stay inside a parked car can be dangerous. For example, the temperature inside your car on an 85 degrees day can reach 102 degrees in only 10 minutes. In 30 minutes, the temperature will reach 120 degrees–and that's with the windows slightly open. A dog can only stand temperatures like these for a very short time before suffering heat stroke, irreparable brain damage or death.

At the beach there are also considerations you need to keep in mind. According to the Humane Society, dogs should not be taken to the beach between 10 a.m. and 4 p.m. That is when the sun's rays

are the strongest and dogs are the most susceptible to heat stroke. If you plan to bring your dog with you to the beach, rent an umbrella to help keep him cool. Keep him off the hot sand; the pads of a dog's feet have just as many nerves as human feet. So if the sand feels hot to you, it will feel hot to your dog.

Dogs love to romp in the surf with a disc, but saltwater is not for drinking. Be sure to bring fresh water from home for him. Saltwater also can dry his skin, so

A child's wading pool is great for cooling off.

84

bathe your dog with a mild shampoo when you get home. This will also help remove the embedded sand from his coat. Again, don't forget to remove your dog's flea collar (if you use one), before heading out to the beach.

In summer when the temperature is high, you might consider reducing the amount of practice time and increasing the number of sessions to comfortably maintain or improve your dog's level of skill. You may find it wise to work out in the early morning or late evening to take advantage of the cooler temperatures.

1992 World Runnerup Greg Tresan and Jumpin' Jess practice year round.

Depending on your dog's coat and amount of exposure to the elements he will be more or less inclined to enjoy being outside in the winter. Winter workouts can be fun but check with your veterinarian first so that you can keep in mind the potential dangers like temperature extremes, salt and ice. Too much play in the cold can damage your dogs feet while sidewalks that have been salted to melt ice (and snow) will burn them.

Talk to your veterinarian about how much food and water you should give your dog and when you should feed him. Most dogs enjoy playing with discs so much that they don't know when to stop, so you must be the one to exercise judgement and restraint. Wait at least two hours after doggie mealtime before serious exercise and don't feed or force fluids immediately after a workout. If he is really panting, give your dog only small amounts of water or ice cubes or he'll drink too much too quickly and get sick. Ideally, give him some time to cool off first. If you are near a lake or a pond, a quick dip in the water will usually cool a dog off nicely.

Frisbee Familiarization

As I have said before, initial Frisbee training can begin when a dog is two to three months of age. I began training Wizard and

Magic at this age by using a disc as a food dish. Doing this made them feel comfortable around it. However, do not let your dog play with a disc or use it for teething on his **own.** After your dog eats from it, put it away until the next meal or play session. There are plenty of other chew toys that you can give him. Your dog must learn that the disc is only used for *special occasions.* You don't want your dog to chew anything laying around because it's expensive and could be catastrophic if, like me, you collect rare, irreplaceable discs. Also, younger canines will sometimes chew and swallow small pieces of flying discs. This can represent a danger to the health of your pet.

Tracking

Tracking is simply the ability to follow a moving object. With dogs, it's instinctive and natural, but it does take time to develop. An example of tracking in human development is a child's ability to catch. At first it looks like the child is closing his or her hands randomly and will never catch anything. With practice, their tracking improves and they can start to predict where a moving object will be for successful catches. A puppy not only has a short attention span, but no tracking skills. If you throw something over his head, to him it simply disappears. Tracking is a skill which takes time to learn and develop.

You can help your puppy's development by rolling a ball, disc or favorite chew toy back and forth in front of him. You also might toss

These photos of World Finalist Susan Summers and her puppy Kip illustrate some of the basics: Feed your dog out of a disc, play light tug-of-war, tease him, roll the disc on the ground, and let him know that this is a toy to be enjoyed together.

it up in the air a small distance and make sure that your dog follows the motion with his eyes.

Wizard would like for me to add that cats are also good for tracking. To him, cats are just discs with fur and he always knows the exact whereabouts of our two felines.

Canine Disc Basics

Do you have to start with a puppy? No, if your dog is an adult dog who enjoys chasing sticks or playing with a ball you can transfer his energy and enthusiasm to the disc. Starting with an adult dog can take weeks or months depending on prior training, conditioning and desire.

After introducing your adult dog or puppy to the pleasures of eating his meals out of a disc, move on to a light game of keep-away. I recommend that you not play tug-of-war with your dog and a disc because it encourages a *hard mouth*; a bad habit of chewing through the disc. Still, I use this concept gently when starting out just to show your dog that it's OK to grab the disc in his mouth. Early training can be done with standard three to nine inch plastic or fabric discs.

Keep-away is used to introduce the element of motion to a dog's game. First tease your dog with the disc by moving it quickly back and forth in front of his face and feet. Get him to grab at it and let him play a light tug-of-war before you make him release the disc. Then slide the disc upside-down across the floor a short distance to encourage his chasing instinct, remembering to always praise him! Your dog might first look at you horrified that you could throw away his food dish. Then he may dash after it to chase it and protect it. Sometimes he will bring it part or all of the way back. If so, give him lots of praise and encouragement. At first, it isn't important that any of these throws be far or fast, just that they're moving. In the early days, Wizard would usually chase my throw, occasionally grab it and rarely bring it back.

After a few sessions your dog will start to feel comfortable with this, so you might began to use a non-food disc and thus it becomes a game to him. Continue with these exercises until he has the *play-time* idea and enjoys the game. Whenever you refer to "*Frisbee*" or "*Playing Frisbee*" use a very animated, upbeat, happy tone; that way it will seem like a special game. For example, "*Wizard, do you want to play FRISBEE?*"

Once your dog is comfortable with chasing and grabbing throws, it is important to teach him to come back to you. A good way to get your dog to understand what you want him to do is to attach a long line to his collar for a play session. After he chases down the disc, call him. If there is any hesitation, gently snap the cord, like a tug on a leash, to get his attention. If this doesn't work, then gently pull him all the way back while praising him for desirable behavior. Never yell at him while you are doing this even if you have to pull him all the way in. Otherwise he will get the idea that he is doing something wrong and won't want to come to you. Do this until your dog comes back all the way on his own, but don't worry at this point if he doesn't bring the disc back. Once your dog has mastered this lesson, try it off-leash. Repeat this frequently for short periods of time until he gets the idea. This exercise also can be done indoors initially and later when your dog is responding consistently, outside. Make sure that all of your off-leash work is done well away from roads and other dangers and distractions.

Don't worry about your dog coming to you without the disc until he is an enthusiastic player. In the meantime you can continue his training with a handful of discs. Later, if your dog comes to you without the disc, you need to move to a small enclosed area to teach him retrieval. (Wizard started this way.) Get your dog really excited and then make a short throw. He will catch it and drop it without bringing it back and look expectantly at you. Tell him to get the disc, then walk over to it and roll it a short distance. Eventually, he will most likely come over to it and pick it up and bring it a short distance to you. Be liberal with your praise for even the slightest improvement in your canines retrieving efforts.

At times your dog may try to play a form of keep-away to get you to chase him for the disc. **Never** play this game! Dogs are pack animals and in the wild there is always one leader. You must become your dog's leader. That is the only way he will consistently listen to you and do what you want. Naturally, you will be put to an occasional test, so be prepared to re-educate him if he has a *keep-away* relapse. For instance, after becoming proficient at Frisbee play, your dog might suddenly get the urge to play keep-away instead of bringing it back. Don't ever let him get away with it! Get out the long line, attach it to your dog's collar and work out with him until he remembers what is proper behavior. You'll be amazed how quickly he *remembers* his lessons. Also, you might try turning your back on a canine that is trying to involve you in a game of keep-away. Usually, the canine will understand that he must return the disc to you in return for your continued involvement in disc play.

Warm-Ups

I have rarely heard people speak about warming up their dog before exercising. In dog training you can't say, *"Give me five jumping jacks to begin."* Still, I believe it's a good idea to start out slowly and not make your first throw too far or encourage your dog to jump too soon after commencing play. You might like to begin by taking a brisk walk with your dog on lead. Then with a disc proceed to some short throws and rollers. Finally, hold the disc over his head to get your dog to jump and stretch his leg muscles.

Catching

This step comes after you have had continued success with getting your dog to chase rollers and sliders.

When training your dog to catch the disc, there are a few requirements to keep in mind. First, to be successful you have to increase your dog's excitement level. Tease him with the disc using tug-of-war, keep-away, rollers and upside-down sliders. He must **want** the disc. Depending on how quickly your dog progresses, and if you started with a pup, he might be four to five months old before he starts catching. If you are working with a puppy he will probably still have his baby teeth. Use a small disc like a Pocket Pro (three inch diameter Frisbee or Fabric disc). Kneel down in front of your dog and get him very excited by waving the disc around his face lightly tapping him on either side of his nose and moving it from side to side. Then flip it gently to him. He instinctively will try to catch it. If he does, praise him like there is no tomorrow. If not, do not let him have it on the ground. Use one hand to prevent him from getting it and the other to pick the disc up. He only gets to touch it if he grabs it out of the air.

Once your dog starts to catch the disc and learns that catching

Here Laurie Berkin and her puppy Scout demonstrate a long roller leading up to a short successful catch.

is the game, move on to using several discs instead of one. Then flip them to him one at a time. When he begins to get fairly proficient at this, start to flipping them to one side or the other. By doing this, you force him to move to the disc. He will catch one and then look for the next. This will accomplish a few goals: It will give him practice catching, it will prompt him to think about moving to the disc and it will get him used to working with multiple discs.

Next, work on upside-down and short vertical throws. After that, you need to move on to longer, more difficult throws. Once your dog can catch a particular kind of toss, try starting with him at your left side. Throw a leading toss about three feet to your right so he has to move to the disc. Remember to allow the dog to maintain eye contact with the disc. Once your dog succeeds at catching short throws you can progress to longer and longer attempts.

Finally, the way to get your dog to run, jump and catch is to hold the disc above his head. Your dog will naturally jump up for it. The jump should be short and low at first—inches, not feet. Let your dog's

World Finalists John Misita and CJ.

first leaping catch be successful by letting him take the disc out of your hand. At first the disc can be angled toward the dog, but after he masters this, keep the disc level or parallel to the ground (giving your dog the same perspective of the disc that he would have if it were flying). The next step is to let go of the disc as your dog jumps up for it. This makes him move with the disc to catch it. From there, move the disc from side-to-side and have your dog follow it until you make a short, three-foot throw. Gradually increase the length of your throws as his expertise increases.

Another exercise that you might want to try is to take your dog along while you play with a Frisbee disc with a friend. Encourage him to run back and forth and try to intercept your throws. Make sure he gets one occasionally and give him plenty of praise. Remember, this is just to be used as a supplemental exercise, otherwise you could give your dog a bad habit of stealing other people's discs and therefore becoming a pest.

Jumping

Most veterinarians recommend dogs don't **train** to jump until after a year of age due to the fragile nature of young bones and joints. This means that jumps your dog chooses to do on his own are probably fine. When you begin training to jump, hold the disc higher than he can usually goes. Make sure that it's just high enough for him to reach and as soon as he can reach it at one height, continue to gradually increase the height. Remember to hold the disc parallel to the ground and a few feet away from the dog. To reduce the possibility of injury avoid having your canine jump straight up for the disc. Don't tease him by overdoing this. Three good jumps before each throw is enough to develop leg strength and jumping ability.

Some dogs will wait for the disc to come down rather than jump up for it. One way to work on this is to attach a disc to a pole with string (like a fishing pole) so that you can swing it away from your body. Then tell your dog to get it. This way you can move and control the height of the disc which forces your dog to leave the ground for it. Gradually increase the height of the disc in practice. Praise him when he leaves the ground; later use a word like *"Jump"* when he does it so that you can use the same word in practice to reinforce the process.

A good method for developing your dog's form was told to me by J.P. Rees. Have your dog jump through a Hula Hoop. This will encourage your dog to pull his back feet up and in when he is airborne.

1989 World Champion Jeff Perry demonstrates a double-disc front flip to a catch of Gilbert in Tokyo.

Advanced Training

Once the basics are mastered, you will probably want to attempt more difficult tricks with your dog. Dogs should be ready for advanced tricks at 6 to 12 months of age. However, for serious jumping tricks or vaults wait until your dog is physically mature. When in doubt, check with your veterinarian. Even then, use common sense and don't push your dog to unsafe heights especially when vaulting.

There are many ways to train the following tricks. I am going to explain the most common methods. However do not despair if you can't get your dog to do them, just continue and try to figure out different approaches til one works. Since the movements involved in advanced tricks can sometimes be complex, you might find my companion video, *Frisbee Dogs: Training Video,* which visually covers many of the tricks in this book, to be helpful *(See Appendix).*

Basic Training Positions

Most of the tricks taught here begin from what I call basic training positions. Both positions can be done standing or kneeling. Later, after you have mastered a trick you can experiment using different starting combinations or positions. The side basic training position is where you face forward and your dog is three to five feet to your side so he is facing you but perpendicular to your

J.P. Rees and Standard Poodle Einstein demonstrate the basic training position.

World Finalists Tony Frediani and Duke demonstrate a warm up "take."

body. A word of caution for doing arm, thigh or leg-over tricks: always extend the body part that is closest to your dog. This affords you some physical protection.

The front basic position is where you are facing forward and your dog is facing you about three to five feet away.

Take

Although you will not directly receive credit in competition for a *take,* the concept is invaluable as a versatile training technique. To learn the *take* start your practice session by getting your dog excited about playing. Then hold the disc out to him and say *"Take."* When he goes for it let him take the disc out of your hand and hold it for a moment. Then you can reward him by making a throw. Once your dog will do the *take* on command, you can gradually raise the disc higher and higher until it's over his head. Say *"Take"* and he will jump up and grab it out of your hand. This is also a useful way of warming him up and strengthening his legs.

Later on, this command can be used when you want your dog to

Mouth "take" by Mike Miller and Pro.

94

take the disc out of your mouth, from behind your head and over your leg or for teaching vaults.

Another variation you might want to try is having your dog *take* the disc out of your mouth. At first, hold the disc upside down in your hand about two feet in front of your mouth. Too close and he might be human shy and not *take* it. Angle the disc toward your dog. Tell him to *"Take."* You may have to start by kneeling and then gradually elevate your body building upon successful attempts. For the actual mouth *take,* rest a clean, dry disc upside down in your mouth. You'll find that it is much easier to hold upside down. Depending on how tall you are and how good a leaper your dog is you may need to bend over slightly, so tilt your head sideways so that the disc is angled toward your dog, and tell him to *"Take."* Although you are facing forward, watch him from the corner of your eye and when he jumps let go. Do not wait until you think it's the right time or until you feel him. If you do there will be a large collision and you will be the loser. Most dogs have much stronger jaws and teeth than we do, so be careful with this trick. It is better to err on letting go on the early side than late.

One interesting variation on this mouth *take* is done by 1989 World Champions Jeff Perry and Gilbert. Instead of a static standing trick Perry begins by running sideways toward Gilbert as Gilbert is running toward him. Then at the last moment, Gilbert *takes* the disc from Perry's mouth. The timing on this trick is critical because there is little room for error.

Another variation on the mouth *take* is making a *hoop* with your arms (they don't have to touch) and having your dog jump through them to *take* the disc out of your mouth. For large dogs the hoop created can be enlarged through the use of discs. If you hold one in your hand the hoop area becomes about nine inches larger than your arms by themselves and if you hold a disc in both hands, 18 inches larger. This will be big enough for almost any dog to jump through.

Reese Blake and Tara demonstrate a two disc hoop.

LONG PHOTOGRAPHY, INC.

95

1989 World Champion Jeff Perry ends his routine with an advanced "take" by having Gilbert jump into his arms. Notice that Perry releases the disc before Gilbert catches it.

Here are a few other tricks you can train employing the *"Take"* command:

- Put the disc on your head (or on your dogs head) and have him *take* it.
- Use the *take* command to have your dog jump into your arms.
- Kneeling or standing put your left arm out from your side; then have him *take* the disc from your other hand as he jumps over your arm.
- Start with your left leg out and have him *take* the disc as he jumps over it. Next add a scissors kick so that your right leg comes up first then your left leg before he *takes* the disc.

Give/Drop

Now that we have covered the *take* command, it's time to mention its equally important counterpart—*give, drop or release*. Some dogs will naturally *drop* the disc at your feet while others practically need to have it pried out of their mouths with a mechanical *Jaws of Life.* Since you may not have access to such a mechanical spreader, it's easier if your dog learns early on in life to let go of the disc on command.

To teach your dog to *drop* the disc on command, have your dog

LONG PHOTOGRAPHY, INC.

You have to remind your dog to let go.

sit three feet in front of you while you are kneeling in front of him. Practice this on leash if necessary to prevent him from running off. Toss the disc to him and let him catch it. Then say "*Drop.*" If he doesn't readily let go, pinch the sides of his mouth against his teeth with your left hand while grasping the disc firmly in your right hand. This is an uncomfortable position for your dog so he will open his mouth and let go of the disc. Praise him and repeat the same sequence until he *drops* the disc on command.

Later with practice you should be able to tell your dog "*Drop*" and he will let go of the disc anywhere on the field. This is helpful in setting up for other tricks.

Over

Once your dog understands the command "*Take,*" you can easily work it into some advanced tricks by combining it with the command "*Over.*" *over* is a versatile trick that can be used in two ways. First, it can simply be a trick by itself. Secondly it can be used as a stepping stone to more advanced tricks. Once your dog knows this command, you can have him jump over your leg, back, head, etc., depending on his leaping ability.

Kneel in the basic side stance. Have one of your knees forward and bent. Give your dog the "*Over*" command. You want to encourage your dog to jump *over* the top of your outstretched thigh. You may have to guide him over the first few times on leash. Once he does this on his own you can have him go over your thigh to take a disc that you are holding. Teaching this to your dog shouldn't be tough because he is just making a little jump. If you want to be creative, you can have him jump over in one direction and then back the other way.

Once he can jump over your thigh, proceed to extending your leg out and then standing up to have him jump over your leg. If you want your dog to jump *over* your back, you may have to start from the side basic position on your hands and knees the first few times and possibly elicit a friend's help in guiding your dog over. Later, from a standing side position all you should have to do is bend over and command "*Over.*"

If he circles around instead of jumping over you, try the following exercise. Put a leash on your dog and kneel facing a wall, tree or fence with your knee against it. Have your dog jump over your knee. The wall will prevent him from running around in front of you, while with the leash you can prevent him from going around behind.

This is a powerful trick, because if you use it as suggested, it is a real crowd pleaser. Having your dog jump over you and doing tricks around you is good for showmanship. However, a word of note for competitors: Since, at this point, the disc is not being thrown or caught, do not use it to excess in competition. It will not add greatly to your score. Later, to really impress your friends and the judges, have your dog jump over you and flip the disc to him simultaneously. For example, as your dog jumps over your outstretched leg, release the disc so that he catches it on the way over. This can be done in many ways and **will** add to your total score if completed successfully.

Start from the basic training position. Extend your left leg, hold the disc over your knee and have him jump over it, taking the disc as he goes. This trick can be expanded so that you do it standing up with your leg outstretched. From this position you can toss the disc instead of handing it to him. Once your dog learns this trick, timing

is critical. You do not want to flip the disc to him once he is in the air because if your throw isn't perfect he can't change his position. Make sure that you say "*Over*" first then flip the disc before your dog jumps. This way depending on where you flip the disc your dog can adjust his jump accordingly. This can be done in either direction.

For a reverse leg over start in a reverse side basic stance. You are now facing forward and your dog is starting to your right instead of left. At first you will need to exaggerate and slow the

TERRI HANSON

Peter Bloeme and Wizard demonstrate a forward "over" the leg catch.

Peter Bloeme and Wizard demonstrate a reverse "over."

trick down. Bend over on your left leg, extend your right leg out behind you and hold the disc with your right hand across your body over your right leg. Then give your dog the command *"Over."* Later, with practice you should be able to assume the reverse side basic position and give your dog the command *"Over."* Then with one motion you will bring your right leg up behind you and flip the disc in the air while your dog jumps over your leg to make the catch. This takes excellent timing on your part; unless you are extremely flexible, you can't twist around to see him take off.

Glenn Medford and Brittany performing the two-handed "over."

The two-handed move demonstrated by Glenn Medford and Brittany is a good example of a two-handed throw and the command "*Over.*" You start in a kneeling position and, using the two-handed throw, flip the disc straight over your head (lowering your head just to be on the safe side), as your dog leaps over you either from in front or from behind to catch the disc.

Finally, the *over* trick can be extended to your catching your dog as he jumps over your leg. This can simply be done where you hold the disc over your leg and command him "*Over*" and as he jumps up and over you catch him. Make sure that one hand goes under his chest and one under his rear so that it's as if you picked him up from the ground or he will be uncomfortable. At first he might fight you a bit but as long as he feels safe and secure, don't drop him, he will get used to this position.

Later you can combine this trick with letting him jump up into your arms to catch the *over.*

Multiples

Current competition rules allow up to five Frisbee discs for a routine, otherwise known as using multiple discs. The true definition of multiples is simply the use of two or more discs at once with your dog. This can be done with several quick, short throws or long floating throws where your dog has time to catch one then drop it as he runs to catch the other. I use the command "*Two,*" so that Wizard will run for the first, make the catch and then immediately look for the next one without looking back at me.

I am often asked how you get your dog to drop the first disc so

Peter Bloeme and Wizard demonstrate vertical multiples. The discs move so quickly that one is usually in the air while Wizard is catching another.

TERRI HANSON

that he can catch another. This is usually not an issue for people who start out with multiple discs, because their dog is usually conditioned to drop one disc and then immediately look for the next. However, for someone who has been using only one disc with his or her dog it needs to be trained.

Here is a sure-fire method: Flip the disc at him and after he catches it say "*Drop.*" If he doesn't release the disc by himself help him to do so. Immediately throw the next disc and continue this process with up to five discs in a row. Your dog will usually catch on quickly.

Here is another variation on this trick: start with two discs, and have your dog at your side to begin. Tell him "*Go,*" and throw one disc short. As soon as he makes the catch tell him to drop it. After he releases the disc, continue with a second longer throw. At first this may be a slow and deliberate two-step process but later it can be speeded up. The final effect is that there are two discs in the air simultaneously and your dog will catch one and then the other sequentially.

This can be a very impressive trick. The easiest way to teach it to your dog is to create a word for a disc in flight (like "*Another*") and to say it to the dog just as he has made a catch of the first throw. Do this on short throws and then progressively work longer and longer. Three-time World Champions Bill Murphy and Bouncin' Boo used this to perfection. Murphy would have three Frisbee discs in the air while his dog ran from one side to the other catching them. The move is not without risk, though, for if your timing is off, your dog simply goes from one miss to another. Precise throwing and timing are essential for this trick.

Multiple Disc Catches

On short distance moves such as takes, overs, front or back flips, it is possible to release two discs at the same time so you and your dog catch the discs simultaneously.

1989 World Champion Jeff Perry uses this trick in his routine with a front flip, while Multiple World Finalists Stan Sellers and Zulu do it differently. Sellers flips two discs in the air simultaneously and his dog catches one in a back flip while Sellers spins and catches the other. He then tosses the remaining disc to Zulu for another flip. My method is using a two-handed throw over my head where I toss two discs simultaneously. As Wizard catches one disc, I tap, then catch the other.

Some dogs will even catch one right after another without dropping them. The best known multiple disc catching canine was Zeuss

Craig Brownell's dog Zeuss demonstrates that eight is definitely enough!

owned by Craig Brownell whose record was nine in his mouth at once. He is listed in the Guinness Book of World Records! I don't think that this can be taught but rather is instinctive on the dog's part. However, it is a good example of finding out what your dog's tendencies are in your training sessions.

Front Flip and Back Flip

The front flip and back flip are variations of the same trick. The flips are identical, though the dog spins its body in different directions. I've simply given each variation a name to differentiate them. In the front flip the dog spins to catch the disc to your left, while the back flip is when your dog spins to your right.

Some dogs will flip naturally on short throws, but to teach these tricks I've found it easiest to start by kneeling with your dog about four feet in front of you. Remember to use lots of praise and reassurance as you follow these steps: Toss the Frisbee vertically to your dog as he stands in front of you. Gradually raise your toss so that he now has to raise up off his front legs. Next, make what appears to be a bad throw over his head and slightly to the side.

If you have him sufficiently excited, he will go for it instinctively. Make sure you spot for him, so that if he comes down poorly you can guide him. For the back flip I use the roller delivery but throw it over his head from the same position using the same progression. Once your dog is catching the front or back flips make sure you say, *"Front"* or *"Back"* before releasing the throw. He will soon learn to associate the word with the trick.

Front Flip: Using a short vertical throw Peter Bloeme makes a toss over Wizard's head. Wizard jumps after the "bad" throw, spins, makes the catch and lands safely.

Back Flip: Peter Bloeme uses the roller delivery to make a throw over Wizard's head. Wizard starts to leave the ground, spins, does the flip and makes the catch.

Tapping

Tapping (some competitors call this tipping) is an original trick I developed which had never been done before in canine competition. I borrowed the idea from human Frisbee disc competition where a person bounces the disc with his or her feet, fingers, elbows, head, etc. Here is how it works: I place Wizard about five feet away and flip the disc upside-down to him over his head. Instead of encouraging him to catch it, I say *"Tap,"* and he hits it back to me with his nose. It is easier to do upside-down because he won't get hit by the lip of the disc. The year after our world championship victory, I elaborated on this one and had him not only tap the Frisbee but catch his own tap. I used the sequence *"Tap-catch."* After seeing this, Frisbee dog owners wanted me to reveal how I taught it. Some even tried to bribe my wife into disclosing it. Others made

103

WALT MANCINI

Peter Bloeme tosses the disc to Wizard upside-down who "taps" it back with his nose.

up all sorts of wild theories. About four years later, I finally saw another dog do this trick.

Since then, I have seen three dog/human teams do this trick so I think its time to let the cat out of the bag (sorry Wizard). As with a lot of tricks, it was surprisingly easy once I figured out how to give Wizard the idea. Until that time it had been incredibly frustrating using beach balls and balloons since Wizard popped both going for catches before I came up with a method that worked. Some people resorted to using muzzles and tying their dog's mouths shut. I felt what was needed to teach the idea was for the dog to feel free enough that he would go for the disc but still be unable to catch it.

Here's how I did it: I sat Wizard about three feet in front of me as I held his collar with my left hand. I would then toss the disc flat to him but over his head. As Wizard raised up on his hind legs to catch it, I would prevent him from catching it with my left hand by pulling him under it. Whenever I did this I said the word *"Tap."* After about a week of this I could let him go for it by himself and he would tap the disc.

1991 World Champion Ron Ellis demonstrates the butterfly throw with Maggy.

Butterfly

As described in the throwing section the butterfly (also known as end-over-end or third world spin) is more easily thrown with the spin moving toward your dog than away from him. It is usually easy to teach your dog the basics of this catch. Have him sit in front of you at a distance of about five feet. Get him very excited, tell him *"Catch"* and flip the disc toward him. At first he might go for it yet look perplexed since it is something new for him. Just repeat this throw without allowing him to get the disc if he misses. After doing it a few times, he will pick it up.

The butterfly catch can be combined with multiples; simply have your dog catch several throws in succession. Like other tricks, this one can be expanded upon. Some competitors will combine this throw and the front or back flip. The thrower tosses a butterfly above the dog thereby causing him to do a flip to catch the disc.

The butterfly can also be done with the disc being spun sideways, called a spinner, in addition to the original end-over-end motion. This new way is especially good in combination with a leg over.

Vaulting

Vaulting is a technique in which your dog jumps off a part of your body such as your back or thigh to get extra height, thereby increasing the difficulty and showmanship of the trick.

The first vault to learn is the catapult. It involves having your dog jump up and off your thigh like a springboard and then into the air to catch the disc. I started teaching Wizard this one by kneeling, holding a disc above my head and then having him jump over my thigh with the *take* command.

Peter Bloeme and Wizard demonstrate the catapult.

You may need to use the technique I mentioned for teaching *over* to prevent your dog from running around you. Get a chair and sit facing a wall (tree or fence) with your knees touching it and put a blanket in your lap for protection. Then, have your dog jump into your lap from left to right. Next, hold the disc up over your lap so your dog has to jump off your lap to get it. Finally, toss the disc up. By this time, your dog will not hesitate to use you as a ramp.

Once you have taught your dog all the basic components of this trick, use it in a performance: Start by positioning your dog to your left. Next, bend your left leg so that your left thigh is parallel to the ground and rest your left foot on the lower part of your right thigh. This will provide you with the support you need. You will resemble a Flamingo at this point. As your dog begins his leap off your bent leg, toss the disc up over your head with your right hand. When done correctly, this trick is a big crowd pleaser. You can easily use this one trick for multiple purposes, for instance I frequently use the catapult to create an interesting ending for our routine. Wizard jumps from my thigh as usual, but instead of tossing the disc, I catch him in my arms and bow.

You will find it easiest to teach (and later to perform), vaulting from a set position and distance. This will provide important consistency.

Other combinations of vaults include tossing the disc in the air, and then bending over and having your dog jump off your back into the air to make the catch. Gary Suzuki and Sam perform a remarkable variation on this one in the form of a chest vault. A word of warning though for competitors who do these type of tricks: a neoprene (diving) vest underneath your T-shirt is a wise investment. I have also seen hunting vests, sweaters and sweat shirts used for protection. For the catapult you might consider a thigh wrap. Otherwise, your dog's claws will scratch your thigh, back and chest, even if their nails are clipped properly.

Cautions on Vaulting

It is important to be aware that vaulting is not a required element in competition. And even so, vaults are scored by technique and form – not height. There are many tricks in a Frisbee dog's repertoire that can be used in place of vaults. Jeff Gabel with Casey and Jeff Perry with Gilbert are modern day World Champion teams who did not do vaults due to their dogs' size, yet they have been very successful in competition.

Some dogs are just too big for vaulting. Generally speaking, once a dog reaches 50-60 pounds it is not a good idea to attempt vaults. Vaulting **can** be dangerous to your dog because he will be coming down from great heights and could land in stressful positions. It can

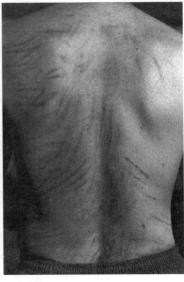

World Finalist Mark Wood prepares his diving vest prior to a demo.

Peter Bloeme exposes the reasons for using protective gear for vaults.

also be hazardous to trainers that are not in good physical condition. Before beginning training make sure you and your dog are in excellent physical condition. After your dog learns how to vault, don't overdo it in practice since vaulting includes much jumping and jarring. A couple of successful modest vaults a week should be sufficient to keep you both sharp.

If you do have your dog vault, make sure you practice in an area clear of objects that your dog could land on. Some competitors like Ron Ellis and Mark Wood like to have their dogs vault, but do so from a low position so their dogs are reaching heights that are within their normal jumping range. Although vaulting is not risk free, vaults with a low trajectory arc safest for your dog. To reiterate, do not use vaulting as a crutch in competition, don't over-practice vaults and finally, do not have your dog vault to excessive heights. You won't get any extra points in competition for doing so and are only taking unnecessary chances with your dog which is frowned upon by the judges.

1991 World Champions Ron Ellis and Maggy demonstrate a catapult sequence, first to Ellis' left and then with Maggy returning to his right. For safeties sake I always recommend raising up the closest leg to your dog. This is shown correctly above left and incorrectly on right where Ellis' left leg should be raised. Since this is done for safety and not technique, Ellis did not lose any points in competition for doing this.

1993 World Champions Gary Suzuki and Soarin' Sam demonstrate a chest vault.

Props

With the exception of uniforms, props are not allowed in competition. However, they can still make for interesting demonstrations. The use of hoops, canes, etc. with a well-trained Frisbee dog can be entertaining and crowd-pleasing.

World Finalist Bandit making a catch.

LONG PHOTOGRAPHY, INC.

LONG PHOTOGRAPHY, INC.

Back Vault Timing: *Both competitors are attempting a back vault. Top: World Finalists Dave Menor and Katie are out of sync because of a late set-up. Menor has waited for his dog to touch his back before releasing the disc. Unless he makes a perfect throw his dog will miss it as no dog can make a mid air correction. Above: Greg Tresan using correct timing to Jumpin' Jess. The disc is already in the air before Jess has touched Tresan's back. This allows her to make any necessary adjustments to catch the disc by jumping further, higher or longer.*

Competition

The first meaningful Frisbee dog contest was held in 1974 at California State University at Fullerton, with radio station KFI and Wham-O as co-sponsors. It was called the *"First Annual Fearless Fido Frisbee Fetching Fracas."* What a classic name! More than 100 canines entered. Alex Stein and Ashley Whippet were considered *ringers* (too professional) and were not allowed to compete. Two of Ashley's good friends, Eldon McIntire with Hyper Hank and Ken Gorman with Schatzie, took the top honors.

The next big canine disc event was a series of demonstrations sponsored by Wham-O at the Rose Bowl during the 1974 World Frisbee Championships. Following that, the events became known as *Catch & Fetch* contests sponsored by Kal Kan.

From 1978 to 1989, Gaines Dog Foods maintained the sponsorship of the world championships for disc-catching athletes. In 1982, the tournament was renamed the Ashley Whippet Invitational in honor of the great Ashley Whippet who had become the epitome of the Frisbee dog. It may be Ashley Whippet's most important legacy. In 1990, Nestlé's Friskies dog food and treats took over the sponsorship.

The Ashley Whippet Invitational, now known as the Friskies Canine Frisbee disc Championships, invites all owners of accomplished canine athletes, as well as novices, to test their disc-

Reese Blake and Tara.

LONG PHOTOGRAPHY, INC.

catching abilities in competition with their pets. The competitions are free and open to all dogs—purebred or mixed, large and small. Friskies supplies all materials gratis to participating community parks, recreation departments and contestants.

Each year, there are over 100 local contests and seven regional finals culminating in the World Finals, held on the Washington Monument Grounds in Washington, D.C.

It is estimated that more than 300,000 dogs and their owners play with flying discs in parks, at beaches and in back yards. Not all people involved in the sport enter the world of competitions, but in 1993 some 10,000 throughout the country did. Even if you don't plan to compete, I recommend going to a few contests with your dog. First, you'll get some idea of what the contest is all about. Second, I know it may seem unlikely, but I'm convinced that your dog will catch on, get excited and learn just from watching other dogs play. I took Wizard to all the contests I could and he ardently watched, learned and cheered (barked) for the competing dogs. Third, it's a good place to network with other dog owners and ask any questions you might have about training. Finally, you may see, or be inspired to create, a trick you hadn't thought of before. To find out the schedule and location of Frisbee dog contests in your area, and current rules, contact Friskies Canine Frisbee disc Championships and start sharing a wonderful experience with your pet. *(See Appendix)*

Sportsmanship and Competition

Winning and losing, in the sport of canine Frisbee, should be **secondary** to the special relationship that you develop and continue to foster with your canine. Competition officials strive to make this sport a fun, family-oriented outlet for man and dog. It provides an opportunity for camraderie, exchange of ideas and enjoyment of sport between those who share similar interests. You get to compete for free in an activity with your dog that requires, more than most dog sports, an equal basis of dedication, skill and contribution between team members.

While it is natural for a competitor to try his or her best and want to win, not everyone can. It's simply a numbers game and doesn't mean you and your dog aren't good or any less entertaining than others. Remember that the most important reason is to have fun—don't lose your perspective.

Not only is judging extremely difficult, but since it is subjective, competitors have a hard time in their own minds differentiating themselves from the competition. There have been instances when competitors have let their egos dominate when they didn't get the scores they thought they deserved. No one enjoys seeing athletes displaying poor sportsmanship.

Judging is a thankless job. It's the least appreciated, yet most difficult role in the sport. The current judging staff at the Regionals, Open and World Finals consists of Alex Stein, Eldon McIntire, Jeff Perry and myself. This experienced staff contains two founders of the sport, five years of world champions and a cumulative experience of over 60 years in the sport.

Monetary prizes for the Friskies Canine Frisbee disc Championships are kept to a minimum because competition officials don't want to promote negative competitive instincts over fun and friendship. In other disc sports, when prizes were increased, the fun, friendship and sportsmanship decreased. I would hate to see that happen in this sport.

The following are the rules as printed in the 1994 Guidelines and Competition Schedule. To clarify some points, I have added my comments in italics.

Agony and Ecstasy of competition: 1991 World Champion Ron Ellis and 1992 World Runner up Greg Tresan.

113

Rules for All Levels of Competition

- Thrower may be any age and either sex.
- All contestants must sign the injury/illness waiver.
- Only one dog/thrower team is to compete at a time.
- Props, of any kind, are not allowed (e.g. hoops, sticks, ribbons, etc.).
- Only the competing dog, thrower and officials are allowed on the field during competition.
- Dog should be put back on leash immediately after competing to prevent scuffles with other dogs.
- Contestants should walk dogs on leash to the on-deck area and field, when instructed.
- Thrower may enter up to two dogs at Community Finals; only one dog per thrower allowed at Regional and Open Finals.
- Official Friskies Frisbee discs *(Fastback Frisbee discs)*, which are supplied to contestants, are the only discs allowed in competition except for dogs under 15 pounds.
- Dogs must be kept on leash at all times, except when competing or practicing. Practice should be held out of range of competition so competitors are not distracted.
- Where required by local ordinance, all participating dogs must have proof of rabies inoculation, and license. Vaccinations for Parvo and Kennel Cough are strongly recommended for all competing dogs.
- Dog owners are required to clean up if their dog takes a "nature break." If break takes place in the midst of competing timing will stop immediately and will resume following cleanup. Points earned prior to the time-out are added to those earned after time is restarted.
- Boisterous challenges of contest officials, abusive language or other inappropriate or unsportsmanlike behavior may result in the contestant's disqualification from further competition in 1994.

Mandatory Disqualification

- Abuse of a competing animal.
- Female dogs in any stage of heat. *Their presence at the site is too disruptive to male competing dogs.*
- Overly aggressive canine behavior.
- At all levels of competition, Friskies Canine Frisbee disc Championships officials reserve the right to change format, competition rules, time allotments, etc., at their discretion.

Community Finals

In order to provide experience and conditioning opportunities for would-be Regional Final and Open Final contestants, more than 100 U.S. Community Finals have been scheduled with no entry fee required.

Community Finals are fun, excellent for conditioning and good competitive experience for you and your dog. Contest officials recommend that you enter as many as possible. Competitors are allowed to register up to two dogs but may only compete with one dog at a time. Community Finals may be scheduled both before and after the Regional and Open Finals.

Community Finals consist of either: A) two 60-second rounds of Mini-Distance or B) one 60-second round of Mini-Distance and one 60-second round of Freeflight. Winners will be determined by adding both round's scores.

If a large number of teams compete, the second round may be limited to the top scorers from the first round, at the local host's discretion.

Community Finals are administered and judged by community-level appointed staff/volunteers utilizing Friskies Guidelines.

Sign up will begin on site 30 minutes before listed time of competition.

Regional and Open Finals

Any dog/thrower team may compete in a U.S. Regional Final for their state of permanent residence. There are no prerequisites for entering a Regional or Open Final, and there is no entry fee required. Only one dog per thrower will be allowed to compete.

In 1994 the Open Final was added to the competition. Any competitor who has not already won a trip to the World Finals, is eligible to compete in the Open Final.

Regional and Open Finals consist of one elimination round of Freeflight. Upon com-

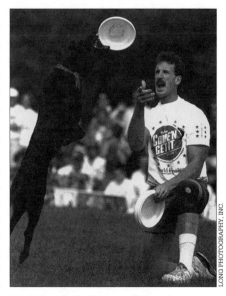

World Finalists Tad Bowen and Hannah.

115

pletion of the Freeflight Elimination Round at each Regional Final, the top six scorers plus the previous year's World Finalists are eligible to compete in the Final Rounds. At the Open Final the top eight scoring teams will advance to the Final Rounds. These rounds consist of one round of Mini-Distance and one round of Freeflight. The new Regional and Open Champion and Runners-up will be determined by doubling the Final Round's Freeflight score and adding it to the Mini-Distance score.

Registration will begin on-site at 9 a.m. at the Regional and Open Finals and is limited to the first 50 teams or until 10:30 a.m. (whichever comes first). *You should give yourself plenty of extra time to get settled before registration takes place.*

No substitutions of either dog or thrower will be allowed at the World Finals. In the event that an (eligible) dog or thrower should become ill or suffer an injury that would, in the judgment of the Executive Director, prevent the caliber of competition expected of a World Finalist, that team will be declared ineligible and the next Runner-up team will go to the World Finals in their place. Regional, Open and World Finals are administered and judged by the Friskies Canine Frisbee disc Championship staff.

World Finalists Bob Evans and Luke.

Mini-Distance Rules

Teams competing in Mini-Distance receive 60 seconds to compete at Community, Regional and Open Finals. However, Mini-Distance at the Regional and Open Finals is limited to only those competitors who qualify for the Final Rounds. *In other words, at a Regional or Open you will be required to score in the top group in Freeflight to get an opportunity to compete in Mini-Distance.*

Only one disc (supplied) is allowed to be used by competitors in this event.

Each contestant may be allowed up to two practice

throws and must advise the time-keeper of the number of practice throws they intend to take, if any, before time begins. This can be done with or without your dog. *Since your dog should already know how to catch a flying disc by this time, I recommend that you take both practice throws without your dog. That will save his enthusiasm and energy. You might also consider making your first throw a short one. That way if it a successful catch you have something you can build on, if not then you haven't sent your dog a long way in vain.*

Timing begins when the disc leaves the thrower's hand. The thrower must always release the disc from behind the throwing line but can freely move about the field at other times, if neces-

1981 World Champions Bob Cox and Belmond at the Rose Bowl.

sary. A throw will not count (and be called as a foot fault) if the thrower steps on or over the throwing line before or during release of the disc. The dog must also be behind throwing line for time to begin (on the first throw only). If the disc has left the thrower's hand before time is called, the throw will be scored if caught. *There are various strategies for Mini-Distance as you can make all long throws, all short throws or a combination thereof. Some competitors will start out with all long throws, as time winds down complete a quick short throw and then try to get a long throw off before time runs out. As long as the disc has been released by that time the throw will count.*

Community Final's scoring is based on this scale for catches. No points are awarded for catches under 10 yards. Between 10-15 yards, one point is awarded if any paw touches ground at time of catch and two points for a mid-air catch. Between 15-20 yards, three points are awarded if any paw touches ground at time of catch and four points for a mid-air catch. Beyond 20 yards, five points are awarded if any paw touches ground at time of catch and six points for a mid-air catch.

117

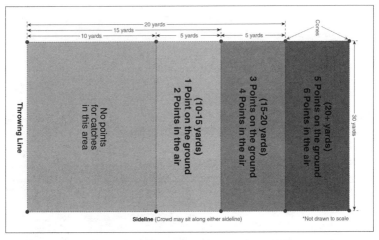

Mini-Distance field layout with Community Final scoring and distances shown.

Regional and Open Final scoring is based on this point scale for catches. No points are awarded for catches under 20 yards. Between 20-30 yards, one point is awarded if any paw touches ground at time of catch and one and a half points are awarded for a mid-air catch. Between 30-40 yards, two points are awarded if any paw touches the ground at time of catch and two and a half points for a mid-air catch. Beyond 40 yards, three points are awarded if any paw touches ground at time of catch and three and a half points for a mid-air catch.

Ideally, a Community Final site should be flat, at least 40 yards long by 30 yards wide, and unobstructed by trees or poles. Grass should be short, with no potholes, and free of debris like glass or rocks.

The field set-up is simple. It is usually best to set up the field across the wind if possible.

Use cones as yard markers. Lining the field with flour *(safer than lime for the dogs)* is helpful, but not necessary. There should be extra room of at least 10 yards on both ends of the field.

There should be adjacent shade trees, if possible, to provide shelter from the sun for animals, their owners and spectators. A nearby water supply for the animals and rest room facilities for throwers and spectators should also be provided.

Freeflight Rules
Freeflight rounds will be 60 seconds at the Community Finals and 60 or 90 seconds at the Regional and Open Finals. Novices (those who

have never competed in a Regional with their dog) will receive 60 seconds to compete while more experienced competitors will receive 90 seconds. *This allows those who are not experienced and who may have limited abilities the opportunity to compete without repeating simple tricks or basic throws.* Timing begins when the disc leaves the thrower's hand. Contestants are encouraged to bring their own perfor-mance music on cassettes

Judging is the least appreciated but most challenging responsibility.

(cued up and properly marked with their name). Only discs provided by the judges (up to five) may be used. No practice throws will be allowed. *Make sure that you practice with multiple discs before you compete with them or you may confuse your dog.*

Only tricks or moves that begin or end with the disc in flight are scored. In other words, the disc must be in the air at some point in order for a move to be scored. Tricks where the disc is handed off to the dog will not be counted. *This means the basic take used in training will not be scored. There are some exceptions like when the dog takes it out of your mouth or you do a trick like resting the disc on you or your dog's head.*

If you would like to try your hand at judging one recommended way to score a routine is to use the "A, B, C" system. This method allows a judge to break down the number of catches and misses. Pick a category and then divide a blank piece of paper up into three columns marked "A," "B" and "C." Every catch and miss is counted in your category. An "A" catch is considered very good (very difficult, a great leap, terrific showmanship or great execution), a "B" catch is average, while a "C" catch is reserved for short simple catches. Mark an "I" for each catch and an "X" for each miss in the appropriate column. This will provide a method of reviewing and scoring each routine. At the end of the routine review your marks to determine a score based on the categorie's criteria.

This method of judging can help differentiate the simple from the

119

●

sublime. For example, it is possible for a competitor who completes a high percentage of easy throws to receive a lower execution score than a competitor who has fewer catches but has a more difficult overall routine. The "A, B, C" system or other equalizing criteria used by the judges, prevent competitors from piling up points with short, easy catches, without overly penalizing competitors who take risks by attempting difficult tricks.

Judges will award points on a 1-10 point scale for each of four categories. *A perfect score is 40. This could be increased up to a total of 48 with maximum bonus points. You do not need to receive a ten in a category to be eligible for bonus points. As a rule, a competitor who receives bonus points will get only one or two out of a total of eight. An average beginner's score with a dog that does basic catching with one disc will be in the 16 point range. Here is a breakdown of the four judging categories:*

Degree of Difficulty

Demonstrated ability by dog and thrower to effectively perform attempted throws/catches of a non-routine nature with consistency. This includes challenging maneuvers, throws with varied spins and catches where the dog does not have eye contact with the thrower and still succeeds, even where second or third effort is required. *Degree of Difficulty is based on how advanced (difficult) as well as how varied the tricks are. A team that does an incredible trick repeatedly will receive a lower score than one with a varied routine. An evenly paced routine is better than one with lots of highs and lows.*

LONG PHOTOGRAPHY, INC.

World Finalists Stan Sellers and Zulu.

Execution

Consistent, smooth completion of maneuvers in a routine that emphasizes teamwork in the progression of throws and catches. *Execution is not solely based on the percentage of successful catches that a dog makes. Consideration is given to contestants who attempt many difficult catches in their routine compared to those who are more cautious. Repetitive, short, easy or multiple throws do not necessarily increase a competitor's score in this category.*

Leaping Agility

Consistency of catches that showcase the dog's style, grace and agility in motion relative to its size. **Note:** The use of vaults, while highly entertaining and often spectacular, should be tempered with consideration for the animal's welfare. Excessive heights, or frequent repetitions of vaults, which employ the

1991 World Champions Ron Ellis and Maggy.

thrower's body as a launching pad, will not increase the possibility of a higher score. *Leaping Agility involves style and grace, as well as how high a dog leaps from the ground in proportion to its size. Up to a point a large dog is generally going to jump higher than a small dog. This is taken into consideration. Vaults do not count towards leaping scores as the dog is getting assistance from the thrower. Leaping agility is judged on average, consistency, style and grace and not on one or two great leaps.*

Showmanship

Demonstrated ability by the dog/owner team to perform unique, novel or even trend-setting maneuvers requiring a high degree of ingenuity, teamwork and consistency. *Showmanship is the ability of the dog and thrower to work together as a team—smoothly and with confidence. Proper disc management is crucial to good showmanship. Competitors who dash madly to retrieve discs and appear haphazard in the manner in which they conduct their routines will likely receive lower showmanship scores.*

Bonus Points

Judges may, at their discretion, each award up to two Bonus Points *(per their judging category)* to competitors with spectacular or innovative Freeflight moves.

121

LONG PHOTOGRAPHY, INC

World Finalist CJ.

Community Finals Awards

All competitors receive Community Award Certificates and official Frisbee discs. Winners and Runners-up receive T-shirts and sportbags.

Regional and Open Finals Awards

All competitors receive Award Certificates, official Frisbee discs and T-shirts. All finalists receive a supply of Friskies canned and dry dog foods and treats, and sportbags. Winners and Runners-up receive trophies and an expense-paid trip to the World Finals. Winners receive a year's supply of Friskies canned and dry dog foods and treats. There are also awards for best novice team and top-scoring *small* dog. *The Novice award is given to the best team whose dog and human have not competed in a Regional before. In other words if the person has competed before but with a different dog or vice a versa they would be considered a Novice team. Small dog is not simply designated by height and size as a small dog can be heavy and a tall dog can be light. However, if your dog is 25 pounds or less it is usually considered a small dog.*

World Finals Awards

All World Finalists receive trophies, official custom apparel, deluxe sportbags and a supply of Friskies canned and dry dog foods. The following U.S. Saving Bonds will also be awarded: World Champion $1,000 U.S. Savings Bond, 1st Runner-up $500 U.S. Savings Bond and 2nd Runner-up $250 U.S. Savings Bond. The World Champion receives a year's supply of Friskies canned and dry dog foods and treats.

World Champions (to present)
'75-'77 Ashley Whippet (Whippet), trainer Alex Stein, Hudson, OH
'78-'79 Dink (Mix), trainer Jim Strickler, Severna Park, MD
'80 Kona (Vizsla), trainer Frank Allen, Phoenix, AZ
'81 Belmond (Labrador), trainer Bob Cox, Johnston, IA
'82-'83 Bouncin' Boo (Mix), trainer Bill Murphy, Lubbock, TX
'84 Whirlin' Wizard (Border Collie), trainer Peter Bloeme, Atlanta, GA
'85 Bouncin' Boo (Mix), trainer Bill Murphy, Lubbock, TX
'86 Kato (Mix), trainer Chris Barbo, Kent, OH
'87-'88 Casey (Labrador), trainer Jeff Gabel, Suffield, CT
'89 Gilbert (Mix), trainer Jeff Perry, Atlanta, GA
'90 Scooter (Aussie), trainer Lou McCammon, Vacaville, CA
'91 Maggy (Border Collie), trainer Ron Ellis, Dallas, TX
'92 Scooter (Aussie), trainer Lou McCammon, Vacaville, CA
'93 Soaring Sam (Mix), trainer Gary Suzuki, Covina, CA

Canine disc competition is spreading globally. Here are Japanese champions Tomiko Yamamoto and her German Shepherd Annie.

Competitor makes dazzling leap at the Rose Bowl.

Ashley Whippet Hall of Fame
(listed in alphabetical order)
Peter Bloeme/Whirlin' Wizard
Jeff Gabel/Casey
Irv Lander
Eldon McIntire/Hyper Hank
Bill Murphy/Bouncin' Boo
Jeff Perry/Gilbert
Donna Schoech
Alex Stein/Ashley Whippet
John Wade
Steve Willett

Contest Promotion
The Bethesda, Maryland-based advertising agency Earle Palmer Brown complimented Irv Lander (Executive Director of the Ashley Whippet Invitational) with some speculative creative promotional advertisements for Frisbee dogs. I couldn't resist reprinting the copy here, with Lander's permission. They have won international acclaim and could well become classic posters:

- **See the only athletes who scratch themselves more than baseball players...**
  Come to this year's Frisbee dog Championship and you'll see some great throwing, running and catching. Not to mention some embarrassing sniffing, scratching and licking.
- **Imagine Michael Jordan with fur.**
  If you think Air Jordan can fly, wait until you catch Air Fido at this year's Frisbee dog Championship. We promise, it will beat anything you'll see in the NBA. By leaps and bounds.
- **Who will lick last year's champion?**
  This year's Frisbee dog Championship promises to be a real battle. So enter your dog today. Even if he doesn't beat last year's champ, we're sure he'll get in a few good licks.
- **See pets perform stupid human tricks.**
  At this year's Frisbee dog Championship you'll see man's best friend perform some of man's best tricks. They'll run. They'll jump. They'll catch.

They Fly Through the Air With the Greatest of Fleas.

The acrobatics at the Ashley Whippet Invitational®
promise to be more daring than ever.
So bring your dog. Bring your Frisbee® disc.
And get ready to watch the fur fly.

THE ASHLEY WHIPPET INVITATIONAL

For more information, call (800) 786-9240, or write 4060-D Peachtree Rd, Suite 326, Atlanta, GA 30319

- **The most fun your dog's had since your leg.**
  If your dog's becoming too attached to you, bring him to this year's Frisbee dog Championship. After all, with all the exercise he's been getting, he might have a leg up on the competition.
- **Beating last year's champion could be a real bitch.**
  If you and Fifi think you're tough enough to topple last year's Frisbee dog Champion, give it a try. But just remember, it's going to take one tough mother to win. And all you have to do is sit. And stay.
- **They fly through the air with the greatest of fleas.**
  The acrobatics at this year's Frisbee dog Championship promise to be more daring than ever. So bring your dog. Bring your Frisbee. And get ready to watch the fur fly.

Flying Dog Products has reproduced the poster shown on the previous page, sized 18" x 24". It is available through their mail order catalog *(See Appendix)*.

World Finalists Chuck Middleton and Boss demonstrate a chest vault.

World Finalist Jendi Holmes and Scotland.

Competition Tips

have competed successfully for 11 years in Frisbee tournaments on my own and more recently with Wizard. In addition, I have been a national canine Frisbee judge since 1985. Along the way, I have developed some tips I feel will benefit anyone interested in competition.

If you are serious about competing, invest in some wet weather gear. This should include a waterproof hat, jacket, pants and boots. For the most comfort year round, get outer garments made from materials that *breathe*. By doing so you will be able to practice with your dog in all weather conditions. You will also be prepared for those competition days that are held during less than ideal conditions.

Formats and Judging

You can do everything right and still receive a poor Freeflight score at a Community Finals. There is frequently a big difference between the experience of the judges of a co-sponsored Community Finals with local hosts and a Regional Event which is professionally staffed by officials with many years of experience judging world class Frisbee catching canines. Even from one Community Finals to another the judging expertise

World Finalist Mark Wood in costume with Zach (who isn't).

will vary widely and is based on the capability, support and experience of the local host.

Out of fairness, contest officials decided that encouraging community hosts to hold Mini-Distance would lead to more consistent scoring because the scoring in Mini-Distance is primarily objective. Still, contest officials received enough comments from contestants and local hosts that they now allow the local host to choose Mini-Distance only or Mini-Distance and Freeflight.

Contest officials occasionally receive complaints from competitors that the Freeflight judging at Community Finals is inconsistent. As you can see, there is no perfect solution; furthermore, local finals are really like Spring training for baseball players and scores are not to be taken seriously. Some events are judged by people who have never trained a dog, never worked with a Frisbee dog and are basing their scores on dog tricks. So be forewarned. What I write here is specifically written for Regional, Open and World Finals contestants and those professionally judged Community Finals.

Know the Rules

I know this one sounds extremely obvious, but many people don't read the rules and consequently receive disappointing scores. Review the current Guidelines and make sure you understand all the rules, not only what is allowed but what is **not** allowed. If you have any questions, have them answered by the officials in charge before the contest begins. Sometimes you can benefit from something that isn't specified in the rules, such as a preroutine.

Preroutine

Time begins in competition as soon as a disc is released, thrown or moved from a set position. A preroutine therefore is a series of moves or actions leading up to the first throw. It is not timed or scored.

I did the first preroutine in competition at the 1984 World Finals where I choreographed our routine so the two of us did simultaneous moves before ever making a throw. We went out and I got down on all fours parallel to Wizard. Then we both sat, laid down then rolled over twice with me ending up next to the waiting discs which I began throwing. This got the crowd on our side, cheering us on before the judging even began.

Put together something short that will make sense for you and your dog. Sometimes it's how you or your dog come on the field, or utilize simultaneous moves, dance, etc. If not done correctly, a pre-routine can hurt your crowd response if it is too long or poorly done. Make sure that anything you do is well tested and rehearsed.

Creativity

There are obvious ways to improve your scores, like practicing Mini-Distance, and indirect ways, such as through musical selection and costumes.

In Freeflight, explore various maneuvers to determine what will look good. Try anything you can imagine and use whatever works. I highly recommend that while you are trying new things, have someone videotape your routine. In review, you may find that some moves you thought looked great were not nearly as impressive as pictured in your mind's eye. The reverse can also be true.

Practice All the Events

I have seen countless competitors work only on Freeflight and then lose a Regional competition because of poor Mini-Distance scores. There is no excuse for this. Remember, if you can lose a Regional in Mini-Distance, you can just as easily win the competition on it.

Before you begin your Freeflight round, count your Frisbee discs to make sure you have the correct amount; five or less. Once you and your dog go out to the competing area, give yourself a few seconds to relax. Don't rush. Check the wind direction, then position yourself and your dog at the right location on the field for your first move. Take a couple of deep breaths before you begin. Once you start don't let your dog take control and lead you. If you react to your dog's actions rather than have him react to you, you will not be successful. You must remain in control of your canine. If you feel as if you are losing control, stop, take a second to regroup and call him over. Your success is a byproduct of your mental attitude. Be upbeat!

Choreography

When I first started attending Community, Regional and World Championships, I was surprised to find many of the best teams didn't have performances that made them look sharp consistently. Keep these things in mind:

- Rehearsed choreography (this doesn't have to be elaborate) is now standard for competitors. This includes performing to music.

Due to the intense pressure during competition you may want to initially write your routine down on a card taped to your wrist or on the Frisbee discs (in a permanent marker like a Sharpie). One Regional competitor Melissa Heeter wrote her routine down in ink on her arm. Unfortunately, she sweated it off in the middle of her routine.

- Working out to the same song every time will make it easier to remember the correct sequence of moves so you don't leave something out. Break your routine into three or four segments and practice them individually as well as consecutively.

- Remember to bring your musical recording with you to the competition. Better yet bring two copies, just in case.

- Make sure your tape is cued and marked properly (right side, wrong side, your name, your dog's name) for the sound engineer at the event.

If you receive low scores, ask the judges how you can improve your standing. You may be overlooking something that the judges can explain. Your dog doesn't have to know many different tricks in order for you to put together a perfectly acceptable routine.

You **do** need to discover how best to utilize your dog's particular skills. For example, if all your dog can do is run straight away from you and make a jumping catch, use some variety. Throw in one direction and then in another, then both mix in short and long throws, and move around. If your dog knows two tricks, incorporate them both by varying speed, timing and distance. Remember that you are being judged as a team and therefore you must look good both in form and uniform.

Appearance/Costumes

Although there is no direct scoring benefit for a professional appearance, don't ignore the psychological effect it can have on a crowd.

You don't have to dress up like it's Halloween. Make sure that at a minimum you are wearing shoes and that your shirt is tucked in. A smartly dressed athlete, in any sport, can exude confidence which can encourage enthusiastic crowd response. This can have a positive effect on you and your canine during a competition. Competitors who are able to get the crowd behind them often turn in performances that far exceed what they could accomplish without this collective emotional boost.

At the 1984 World Finals, all contestants were issued clothing, but they were only required to wear the sponsor's T-shirt in the competition. Some competitors actually chose to wear blue jeans. I competed in a color-coordinated, clean uniform featuring the sponsor's T-shirt, matching shorts, leg-warmers (popular at the time), wrist bands and clean sneakers. Wizard was freshly groomed, and wore his usual black and white fur coat adorned with *paw bands* that I designed for all four legs. By dressing this way we projected a professional image. One good suggestion for paw bands is a material called prerap, which comes in a variety of neon colors.

Music

As with appearance, you will not receive a higher or lower score simply based on your choice of music, musical category or, for that matter, whether you chose to use music at all.

However, here is a scenario to illustrate how music can affect one's score. Let's assume that there are two competitors with identical dogs and routines. The first competes with no music. The crowd watches politely and claps on occasion. Some in the audience pay attention, others talk with their friends or look elsewhere. The next competitor begins with a popular, crowd-pleasing and upbeat tune. The crowd perks up, snaps their fingers, rocks back and forth and taps their feet. Suddenly they become **involved** and **focused.** Their interest is piqued, they want the performer to do well and live up to the energy and excitement of the music. Since the crowd is involved they begin cheering and clapping more so than for the first competitor. This energy and excitement is passed along to the competitor and to the competitor's dog. This gets them more involved in their routine and they push a little extra, try a little harder and perform a little better. Since their performance is better, the judges award them higher scores.

Some competitors have invested time and money to record their own performance music. Although these songs are usually entertaining, competitors are better off taking the time to choreograph their routines and practice with their dogs. Most audiences don't usually notice the specifics of the music and the judges, though entertained, are not going to *score* the music.

It doesn't matter what your music is or what musical genre it is from as long as it has broad appeal, fits your dog and your routine, has an upbeat tempo and that the lyrics or themes involved aren't offensive to a family audience.

Innovation

1989 World Champions Jeff Perry and his dog Gilbert have developed many trendsetting Freeflight moves. Therefore, I felt that it would be a valuable addition to my book to reprint an article written by Perry for the Greater Atlanta Dog and Disc Club newsletter on innovation to provide others some insight in this important area.

"If you sit on your good routine year after year, regardless of how perfectly you execute it, it will soon seem average when compared to the routines of those competitors who are constantly pushing the limits, searching for tricks that have never before been accomplished. Innovation helps to explain how dog/owner teams like Peter Bloeme and Wizard, Gary Suzuki and Sam or Chris Breit and Mattie can appear seemingly out of nowhere and finish in the top one, two or three spots at the World Finals.

"Sometimes, this is as simple as putting a new variation on a familiar move. Better yet are unique new tricks that drop the jaws of spectators and judges alike. You know the ones I mean. The tricks that make you turn to the person standing next to you and say; 'Did you see that?'.

"Innovation requires brainstorming. You must think long and hard about what might be accomplished. Also, you must not be afraid to try new tricks. Bring seemingly disparate elements into play if possible. Many innovative disc tricks utilize elements of ballet or dance. Other tricks have their origin in sports such as soccer, gymnastics or croquet (just kidding, about croquet). Lou McCammon and his World Champion canine Scooter perform a flying reverse kick and catch combination perfected by the great soccer player, Pele. Still other tricks will be the result of a compromise between a trick that you imagine and the realities of the physical limitations of you and your canine. For example, a trick that I developed recently, in which I catch a back-flipping Gilbert, behind my back, is actually a compromise. Originally, I was attempting to catch him after I made a 360-degree spin. Unfortunately, I was unable to spin fast enough to catch him more than 10 percent of the time (Editor's Note: this wasn't all that thrilling to Gilbert). Almost as a lark, I decided to attempt to catch him behind my back. It worked the first time I tried it and, as it turns out, is a more spectacular trick than the original trick I was attempting.

"Do not give up on a good idea merely because you experience limited success at first. Sometimes all that is needed is a slight modification to solve what seems to be an unsolvable problem. Be patient as you experiment with new and innovative tricks, and remember, if

you can imagine it, with a little practice you can probably accomplish it. With hard work, you can perfect it."

Strategy

My best advice is to **have one!** You should be alert, know the rules, choreograph to music if possible, practice, develop a short preroutine, dress appropriately, be aware of weather conditions (especially the wind for throwing direction) and know the order in which you will be throwing. Make sure your music is clearly marked, cued and the correct side identified before turning it in. Be prepared!

Do not let your nervousness manifest itself by overworking your dog at the site before the competition. I have seen many competitors leave their best routines on the sidelines. The day of the contest is not the time to teach your dog anything new. As a team, you are either already prepared or you aren't. A couple of throws should be all that are necessary to warm him up before you go on. Before and after you compete keep your dog cool (or warm) as necessary. For example, if it is a hot summer day, bring an umbrella or tent as a backup to finding a shady spot. If it's hot wet him down to keep him cool. Be smart. Don't bring food or feed him during the competition. Even if your dog is a free feeder he will not starve if he doesn't eat for a few hours.

Concentrate on what you and your dog are good at, but remember that the competition is a disc-**catching** event. Limit any tricks you do that include your dog taking discs directly out of your hand. While good for training, *hand-held* tricks (which were in fashion a few years back) are no longer worth the time because they are not scored. It doesn't matter if your dog jumps over your back, over your leg or twists in the air if all he is doing is taking the disc from you without a throw. On the other hand, if you flip the disc in the air first it will count as a catch and generate a score for you in all the competition categories.

Working with the Media

Since the sport of canine Frisbee is very media-oriented, there are some basic rules to keep in mind during both competitions and exhibitions:

Sponsor: The sport of canine Frisbee is wonderful, fun and exciting, but it wouldn't exist without a sponsor. A sponsor is always looking for publicity; therefore, do your best to accommodate any media requests, as long as they don't interfere with your competition preparations. Maintain a professional demeanor and be supportive of the sponsor in the quantity and quality of your comments.

Competition: While actually competing, do not let a camera-person (still or video) control your actions. I learned this lesson when I was a junior champion. I did anything anyone with a camera wanted at the expense of my concentration. The media is looking for good footage and you are looking for a good score. Sometimes your agendas are the same; sometimes not. A camera-person may ask you to perform before competitions, or between rounds. Since this can tire your dog and seriously affect your performance, you can tell the reporter politely that you will be happy to spend some time with him or her after the contest is over.

You also may find camera equipment or reporters in an area that interferes with your performance, or for some reason spooks your dog. I experienced this during the 1984 World Championships in Chicago. Wizard wouldn't return the Frisbee all the way to me during the mini-distance round. Although the reason wasn't immediately apparent, I later realized that the camera crew behind us—complete with reporter, sound person, camera-person and large tripod, had frightened him. Since a competition is geared to facilitate your best possible performance, you are within your rights to mention any concerns to the officials before you begin. They will understand and resolve the situation.

Exhibition: If you are working with a camera crew, find out what **they** want to shoot. Then help position them in a logical and safe area where they can get that footage. Explain what your dog is most likely to do as he gets warmed up or when he tires. Also mention that warming up, as in any sport, is necessary. Besides the concerns I mentioned above, there are two additional points to keep in mind during an exhibition or private publicity session. Your first responsibility is your dog's **safety.** This might mean positioning a camera crew a short distance away from the action. It should mean refusing to work on asphalt or in extreme heat. Finally, it might mean taking a **break** to rest your dog. Cooperate, but keep your dog's welfare in mind.

General: Anytime you work with the media, always represent the sport and activity professionally in your appearance and in your attitude. Be prompt, courteous and accommodating. It is acceptable to ask if you can have a copy of the photos or video shot, although this may not always be possible. Answer television questions in short, brief *sound bites*. Don't look straight into the camera and be sure to speak clearly. You will find that being a professional with the media (and your fellow competitors for that matter) will take you a lot further than being an egotist or show-off.

1990 World Finals Runners-up Chris Breit and Mattie.

Two-Time World Champions Lou McCammon and Scooter

Travel

ravelling to my first World Finals as a judge seemed to foreshadow things to come for me as I exited from gate *K-9*. Getting to events and demonstrations is typically done two ways: by car or by plane. It is important for you to familiarize your dog with both forms of travel whenever possible, since travel can be stressful for you and your dog. There are many things to consider before hitting the road with Rover.

Kennels and Crates

Get an airline-approved kennel (sometimes referred to as a crate) to serve as a travelling dog house *(see Crate Training in Canine Considerations)*. They can be purchased at a pet store or at the airport. I don't recommend you make the purchase immediately before a trip as you will need to first get your dog acclimated with his mobile home to reduce the stress associated with travelling. Make sure that you clearly and permanently put your name, address and telephone number on the kennel. Do this immediately. The kennel should have a piece of carpet or other absorbent material on the floor along with water and food

Here, 1989 World Champion Gilbert is firmly BOLTED into his modified kennel. The extra security became necessary because Gilbert did not take to a kennel easily. Before his owner's modifications, Gilbert escaped and terrorized Atlanta's Hartsfield Airport.

cups. They attach to the inside of the kennel and normally you don't have to use them.

It is very important to buy the correct size kennel for your dog. Jeff Perry, the 1989 World Champion, called a manufacturer when he started travelling with his dog Gilbert and was told he should buy a kennel that did not allow his dog to stand up. This kind of misinformation is disturbing. The correct size is one that **will** allow your dog to stand up and turn around easily but not so big that he can be bounced all over (unless he is a puppy and you are planning for him to grow into it). Make sure that you get one made for and approved for air travel with adequate ventilation on the sides and ends. They are usually made out of plastic. Also, make sure the container is *doggie-secure* to prevent your little Houdini from escaping at the most inopportune moments.

Once your dog is generally comfortable in it at home, you can simulate the effect of flying by travelling with the kennel in the car or truck. This can be done on short outings until your dog feels secure in it. This is also a lot safer than letting him run loose in the car, since an accident or short stop could cause your dog to go flying.

When travelling, don't overload the kennel with a lot of junk. Do provide bedding and a couple of favorite toys (not discs though). Also, don't feed your dog a few hours before driving or flying. It will only accentuate any likelihood of motion sickness.

Gilbert Takes a Lickin' and Keeps on Tickin'

I wrote the following story for the Greater Atlanta Dog & Disc Club's newsletter. I included it here to demonstrate that no matter how careful you are something can go wrong. Always be careful.

On May 5, 1991 Gilbert, the 1989 World Canine Frisbee disc Champion, was slightly injured in what could be called an automobile accident. Owner/Trainer Jeff Perry and myself along with canines Wizard, Toulouse, and Gilbert, were returning from a half-time performance at a World League Football game in Durham, North Carolina.

Perry and I were flagged down by a vehicle whose driver told us that Gilbert had bounced out the back of the camper top-covered pickup truck approximately four miles back. Apparently Perry's **locked** rear camper-top door must have been jarred open by a bumpy section of I-85 in North Carolina. Gilbert was deposited on the pavement of I-85 at a speed of no less than 65 miles per hour.

A frantic hour and a half long search ensued up, down and around the highway in the rain and impending darkness and resulted in the recovery of the champion from the median strip. When the emergency veterinarian in Concord, North Carolina received our call, she expected that she would have to set Gilbert's bones and patch him up from head to toe. However, luckily Gilbert received only minor scrapes in the accident. Remarkably one week after the accident, Gilbert was cleared by his regular veterinarian to resume his full disc activities.

Said Perry, *"Almost losing my best buddy was a sobering experience. I would advise everyone to be extremely careful while transporting their pets. Take precautions that border on the absurd if necessary."* Also, Perry strongly recommends that your dog have a name tag attached to his collar that lists your current address and telephone number. If the information becomes dated or incorrect, it's time to obtain a new tag. Gilbert now rides up front with Jeff. I ride in the back.

Driving to Distraction

A few years ago I was on the road doing media appearances as part of the Friskies Celebrity Touring Team to promote an upcoming Regional competition. Normally at least two people and dogs perform but in this case my partner Eldon McIntire was too ill to leave his hotel room. Since there were a number of appearances to be made that day, I borrowed his dog Cricket to perform with in addition to my dog, Magic.

The weather that day was hot and humid. To keep the dogs cool we left them in a parked, air conditioned van with the engine running whenever possible. I would take one dog out of the van then switch dogs for the next show. The shows were being shot on the Regional site so there were a number of arriving competitors watching the interviews.

As I was finishing up one show with Cricket, I heard someone say, *"Hey mister, your dog just drove off."* I laughed and headed back to the van, or I should say where the van had been. I found it nearby in a small ditch. Apparently while Magic was waiting, he jumped into the driver's seat and knocked the gearshift into reverse. Competitors who saw this thought at first that it was a publicity stunt, but after knocking down a garbage bin, narrowly missing a school bus, hitting a parked car and rolling into a ditch, Magic convinced them otherwise. Luckily no one was hurt and Magic has since had his learner's permit revoked.

Air Travel

When travelling by air it is best to arrange a *non-stop* flight to your destination. Next best is a *direct* flight, which means that you have one or more stops on your journey but there is not a change of planes. Finally, my least favorite type is the *connecting* flight. You not only have to make a stop in a city that is not your final destination, but you also have to change planes. This means the airline needs to move your dog from one plane to another in a timely manner. As you can well guess, with this type of flight there is a much greater potential for error. You could make the flight and your dog might not make the transfer or you both could miss the next flight out due to a delay or your dog could be sent to some exotic land.

Be aware of commuter flights where the cargo area of the plane is too small for your dog. If this is the case, you may have to drive to a larger airport.

Make sure to notify the airline that you will be travelling with a pet because you'll usually need to make a special reservation for him. At the time of this writing, there is a charge of around $50 each way to fly your dog on your flight. Your dog's ticket cannot be purchased through your travel agent. However, once you have your ticket in hand you can buy your dog's tickets in advance at the airport or airline ticket office. I recommend that you buy a round-trip ticket for your dog as it is easier to go through the process just once for each trip. Due to various state regulations, your dog must also have a travel certificate from your veterinarian that says that your dog is healthy, has the appropriate vaccinations and can travel safely. Only one dog is allowed to travel per kennel.

For trips leaving, travelling through or landing in areas of extreme temperatures all the airlines have rules and requirements. Check with your airline for their specifics. Depending on the weather, for your dog's safety you may or may not be allowed to travel on the flight which you had planned. Keep this in mind when you make that reservation. For example, if it is high temperatures you are concerned about, you might want to leave, connect or arrive early or late in the day.

If for some reason you can't travel on the same flight as your dog, he can be shipped as air cargo or freight. I have had to do this a few times due to conflicting, business-related travel. You need the same forms and kennel, but more cash. The crate is not considered excess baggage but rather as *freight,* so you are charged by weight. You will need to go to the cargo/freight terminal of the specific airline your dog is flying. This terminal is usually found in more remote areas at airports. Make sure you check the flight times before you get to the airport so you can let them know when you want your dog to travel. Plan to arrive at least two hours before the flight. That will give the airline time to put your dog on the correct flight. Make sure that you have someone pick him up at air cargo **immediately** on the other end. This kind of shipment is fairly common and the airlines are good about keeping the dog in a cool or heated room as appropriate. Many thanks to various humane associations for lobbying to bring about such professional care.

Air travel in the U.S. is pretty straight-forward compared to travel overseas. Some island countries, like England, require that you quarantine your dog for six months. Obviously, this would be ridiculous to go through unless you were permanently moving there. Our travels to Japan required a two week quarantine. Always check with the airline you will be travelling on for the most up-to-date information on the necessary credentials and certification.

When I flew to Berlin, Germany with Wizard for the NFL's American Bowl, I went to the extent of getting German documentation for my veterinarian to fill out. Not one person checked our forms but you can bet they would have if we didn't have them. I found it interesting that coming back from Berlin, Security X-rayed Wizard's kennel (without him in it).

Accidents and mistakes can happen and travel is not without risk. Many dog owners have concerns and fears about flying with their pets so I will try to alleviate as many of those as I can. Since I travel extensively on Delta Air Lines, I contacted them for more specific information about travelling with a dog. They were also kind enough to give me a *backstage tour* of something Wizard and Magic know quite well, in order to take the photographs used in this chapter.

On the appointed day Wizard and I drove to the airport and went through the whole process as if we were going on a trip. Wizard was confused because this time I went with him and he didn't fly. I learned that there was a lot that I didn't know, despite being a frequent traveler. Many thanks to Delta Air Lines for its help in providing this information.

The Flight Explained

Assemble your dog's kennel and make sure it is securely latched and all bolts are tight before putting him in it. Make sure the kennel is marked with your name, address and telephone number in several

When your dog gets checked in, make sure he gets the proper destination tags.

Next, your dog is transported by cart to a waiting area and then out to the plane.

At the plane, your dog will be put on a conveyor to the pressurized cargo area.

Here, Wizard is almost in the plane where his kennel will be stowed.

Baggage is placed around his kennel, without blocking the air flow.

Your dog will meet you at the oversized baggage claim area upon arrival.

places and make sure the correct destination claim check is attached to your ticket envelope. Check your dog in at the ticket counter.

Your dog begins his journey by entering security through baggage. He is then placed in a waiting area before being taken out to the plane. Pets are loaded last and taken off first, though they usually arrive at oversized baggage claim after the other baggage.

The area in the aircraft in which your dog travels is pressurized, heated and cooled as necessary, just like the plane's passenger cabin, but no meals or drinks are served and no frequent flyer points are awarded.

After arriving at your destination, find out where oversize baggage arrives and wait there for your dog. If he doesn't show up right away, don't panic. Some airlines put the baggage out first and then bring out the dogs. I have waited as long as 45 minutes to have Wizard or Magic delivered to me. It is a good idea to let the airline personnel know you are expecting a dog. If there is no sign of him, go to the airline office and report it. They will look on the plane and in the baggage area, and if there still is no sign of him, they will then put a trace on him for you.

Food and Water

When travelling, make sure you take along an adequate supply of dog food. Even if his favorite food is widely available, you don't want to have to go looking for it upon arriving after a long trip. I always bring enough food for an entire trip because it is easier than going out to find some. Because of the food, my luggage is generally heavier going out than it is coming home (which is usually advantageous for those travelers like myself whose spouses love to shop 'til they drop).

Some people take along water from home for fear their dog's digestive systems may not be comfortable with local water. I have not found this to be a problem. Even in Germany, Wizard, Ashley Jr. and Gilbert drank local water with no adverse affects. By the way, as I mentioned earlier, ice is sometimes better than water when your dog gets overheated. It gives your dog a chance to cool down slowly without becoming waterlogged.

Hotels

Most people assume that it is difficult to find a hotel that will accept dogs. This is simply not so. For example, most Marriotts, Holiday Inns, Howard Johnsons, Motel 6s, Ramada Inns and Red Roof Inns, to name just a few hotel chains, will accept your canine with you. For your protection, when booking a room at a large chain ask the hotel or main reservation number whether your dog is allowed in that specific location. This does not give you carte blanche to let your dog mess up the room or keep the neighbors awake by barking. As a responsible pet owner, you should train your dog to be obedient and well behaved before you attempt to take him travelling with you. You may get some strange looks from time to time from people who are not as well informed. When checking in, immediately put the *do not disturb* sign on the door to prevent people from barging in on your dog and possibly freaking out. Also, immediately pick up any welcome food or candy that is sitting out. Watch out for chocolate candy since it is poisonous to dogs.

There were a few times I had to sneak my dog into a room against the hotel or state's wishes. Once, I was doing shows in Pennsylvania and the weather was awful. I had to stop driving and find a hotel. None in the immediate vicinity allowed dogs, and the temperature fell below zero so I couldn't leave Wizard in the car. I thought I would be able to sneak him in the rear entrance until I noticed that the hotel had video cameras on all the entrances. With no other option, I had to take extreme measures. I stuffed him into a large, hard-sided suitcase and carried him into the room. The next morning it was considerably more difficult coaxing him back into my suitcase, but *sometimes you have to break the rules.*

World Finalist Zach.

146

Collecting Discs

Several years after I had started competing, I came across an unusual hobby: I found many competitors collecting flying discs. Quite a few of them had 50 to 100 discs (some many more) hanging on their walls, stuffed in boxes and strewn all over. I thought this was a pretty stupid practice—at first.

I actually became a collector unintentionally. I would get a tournament model here and there, then I would pick one up because it had a pretty logo. I started hanging them up neatly on the wall. Without knowing it, I had become an accumulator, or rather, a collector. Before I realized it, I owned over 50 discs. For a year after that, I went wild and bought, traded and acquired anything that was flat, round and could fly.

At that point, I ran out of wall space, so I designed and built special shelves to hold my favorite discs vertically—like record albums. This way, I could display more discs per foot of wall space. I put the rest into storage. As with all collectors, I eventually reached a satu-

World Finalist Gary Gomes and Kelly.

Year: *1976*
Color: *yellow*
Imprint: *red*

Year: *1977*
Color: *yellow*
Imprint: *black*

Year: *1978*
Color: *white*
Imprint: *blue*

Year: *1979*
Color: *white*
Imprint: *red and black*

Year: *1980*
Color: *white*
Imprint: *red*

Year: *1981*
Color: *white*
Imprint: *red and black*

Year: *1982*
Color: *clear*
Imprint: *red and gold*

Year: *1983*
Color: *red*
Imprint: *gold and white*

Year: *1984*
Color: *white*
Imprint: *blue*

Year: 1985
Color: yellow
Imprint: blue

Year: 1986
Color: red
Imprint: blue and white

Year: 1987
Color: yellow
Imprint: blue and red

Year: 1988
Color: yellow
Imprint: blue and red

Year: 1989
Color: yellow
Imprint: blue and red
(northwest region only)

Year: 1989
Color: yellow
Imprint: red and black
(far west region only)

Year: 1989
Color: yellow
Imprint: blue and red

Year: 1990
Color: white
Imprint: blue, black and red

Year: 1991
Color: white
Imprint: blue, black and red

Year: 1992
Color: white
Imprint: blue, black and red

Year: 1993
Color: white
Imprint: blue and black

Year: 1994
Color: white
Imprint: blue and black

ration point where I had to choose a specialty (limiting myself to one color, model, size, type, etc.) I chose to concentrate on Wham-O Frisbee discs (mainly Professional Models), plus the unusual. Some of my unusual discs are made out of cloth, some make sounds when thrown, some light up (not just glow), and some have strings attached so they return to the thrower. My collection now numbers in the thousands.

I'm sure collectors of all things share the same dream I had—that of accidentally stumbling across an amazing trove of whatever it is they collect. I dreamed about walking into an old toy store and while digging around in the back finding some antique discs hidden away in an old, dirty, dusty box. For me, this dream actually came true. However, it wasn't an old toy store but a new gas station.

While driving all night on a demonstration tour, I pulled into a brightly lit, modern Shell gas station at 2 o'clock in the morning. I pumped my gas and went inside to pay. As I walked groggily to the counter, I realized

Unique U1 Saucer.

there was something unusual about the colored plastic hubcaps I had observed on top of the cigarette machine. Upon closer inspection, I discovered they were *Unique U1s,* antique discs I had never seen or heard of. Despite my excitement, I managed to casually ask the man at the counter where on earth he had found those old discs. He told me they had been sitting around his old gas station for years and he had just moved them to the new station to get rid of them! After negotiating a discount for *taking them all off his hands,* I bought them for very little.

Why would a normal, reasonably intelligent person choose to collect discs? Because discs can be pretty, colorful, interesting, unique, historic and certainly conversation pieces. More importantly, they usually represent experiences and memories of the sport and a fun time in life.

Unfortunately, from a canine Frisbee collector's standpoint, there were some years where no year was imprinted on the discs used in competition. This has created some confusion in the canine disc collecting community. Therefore, I have pictured all the Fastback Frisbee discs that have been used in national competition on pages 148-150.

If concealed Frisbee discs were illegal, Larry Taylor would be in jail.

1993 World Champions Gary Suzuki and Soarin' Sam.

Wizard's Competitive Experience

Wizard's first tournament was in 1984 at the Ashley Whippet Invitational (AWI) Regional in Boston, Massachusetts. He was just a little over one year-old at the time.

I had been working in the Boston area the week preceding the tournament and it rained every day. The day of the contest, Saturday, June 2, was no exception. When I woke up it was pouring and I headed out to see what the situation was at the tournament site. When I arrived, I saw Executive Director Irv Lander and Chief Judge Alex Stein waiting patiently in a parked car at the site. They said that due to the inclement weather the competition was postponed until Sunday.

Sunday surprised everyone by being a beautiful day—sunny and clear. I arrived early before anyone else and warmed up with Wizard. The next people to appear were the park department personnel accompanied by Lander and Stein.

Nancy Mullen of the *Christian Science Monitor* wrote on November 20, 1984:

"The stands are bristling with a lively mix of fans. A dozen athletes of various stripe and spot sit panting in anticipation. From his perch on the top bleacher, a miniature dachshund yaps out his impatience.

"The Ashley Whippet Invitational is about to begin.

"Gathered here on the

Peter Bloeme with Wizard doing a backflip.

153

Boston Common are dogs from all over the region who will vie for the title of champion canine Frisbee-catcher. To win, a dog must jump higher, run faster and catch more flying discs than any other contestant (allowing for differences in potential among the breeds). And he or she must do it all quickly, with style, grace and showmanship. In each of three rounds, the dog/owner teams will have only 45 to 90 seconds to show the judges their stuff.

"Out on the field, a little black and white border collie named Wizard is eying the plastic disc in his master's hand. 'Ready, Wiz? You're gonna JUMP,' the young man commands. Wizard's eyes flash and every muscle is a quiver. He's obviously ready. With a flick of the man's wrist, the disc goes soaring and the dog hurls himself after it like a bean out of a slingshot. For a brief moment, dog and disc float six feet above the ground. Then, with a half-somersault in midair, the collie grabs the saucer, hits the ground running and races back to his owner. After a quick pat and 'Good catch, Wiz,' he's off and flying again. Back in the stands, the fans—both human and canine—are exuberant. A black and white pooch named Erin is barking and leaping up and down in frenzied imitation of the action going on out in the field, while the toy dachshund makes his own observations on the proceedings."

The tournament was essentially a two-dog race between Wizard and a mixed breed named Isis. Mike Smith, owner of Isis and 1982 World Finalist, always impressed me with his vaults and consistency. In fact, Smith demonstrated to me early on in my experiences with Frisbee dogs that only your imagination limits the tricks that you can perform with your canine. To me that was quite an inspiration. Anyway, both our dogs scored the same in distance. When Freeflight came, Wizard and I performed well enough to win. The competition was a tremendous learning experience for me. Winning made Wizard and I the Northeast Regional Champions and earned us an invitation to go to the World Finals in Chicago that September.

World Finalists Mike Smith and Isis provided the author inspiration.

Preparing for the World Finals was one of the hardest things I have ever done. Wizard and I practiced intensely the month before the tournament. My long-time friend Jackie Bernard helped in practice by timing and videotaping us. Afterwards we would critique the routine on video. I really benefited from being able to watch the routine from a different perspective. Things I thought looked good really didn't and vice versa.

By the time we left for Chicago, we were well prepared. Wizard and I would begin side-by-side about four feet apart and then simultaneously sit, lie down and roll over twice before starting the throwing and catching segment. I planned short and long throws with the disc right side up, upside down and vertical. In addition, Wizard would do multiples (more than one disc), execute back flips, tap/hit the disc back to me with his nose (first time ever to be seen in public) and jump over my leg and back. I wore a designer top with red shorts, new sneakers and red wrist bands. Wizard wore a red bandanna with red paw (wrist) bands, a Peter Bloeme original. Finally, for music, I selected a song from the movie *The Wiz* to accompany our routine, with *Ghostbusters* as a backup.

The following article by Paul Sullivan was published in the September 7, 1984 *Chicago Tribune:*

"Besides the now-standard doggie backflips, spectators can expect some original moves never yet seen in the annals of disc-catching dogs.

"'We've got quite a few tricks in store,' countered Peter Bloeme of Brooklyn, a former World Frisbee Champ, who, with his dog 'Wizard,' is attempting to become the first pair of human/animal Frisbee champs. 'I'm not at liberty to mention any of them now. It's a dog-eat-dog world, you know.'"

After a long and

JEFF CARLICK

Peter Bloeme and Wizard show a reverse roller.

uneventful drive from New York City, we arrived in Chicago a day early so Wizard could get used to the site and climate conditions, the most serious of which turned out to be the unpredictable, gusty, 20-mile-per-hour winds! Once we arrived, I had new cause for concern: Wizard had developed diarrhea, and I was afraid it would weaken him. I found it hard to eat and sleep because of my anxiety over Wizard.

The tournament was to take place over the course of two days. The first round of Freeflight and Mini-Distance was scheduled for the morning and the second round of Freeflight for the evening of the first day. The top five dogs would advance to the Finals which were to be held the following day at Comiskey Park, home of the Chicago White Sox.

Day one, Friday, dawned clear, hot and windy. Not surprisingly, there were few spectators, as it was a business day. I felt our first round was a little shaky. Near the end of our routine, I made a throw that Wizard tipped (brushed) and caught. On the way back he suddenly stopped to smell the ground—he had never done that before. I ran over to him and tried to finish the routine with a flourish, but time had run out.

The next event was Mini-Distance. I knew that this event could very well decide the outcome of the competition. The site was laid out so that we could throw in either of two directions. Because of the gusty winds, I spent a lot of time practicing to try and figure out the best direction from which to throw. I decided to go from the far end into the wind. We began and Wiz made a good first catch, but instead of bringing it all the way back to me, he stopped about 20 feet away. I didn't realize it at the time, but a camera crew behind me spooked him. Anyway, I went out, got the disc, ran back and threw. Because of this delay I rushed, making a bad throw that Wizard couldn't catch. Since we only had 60 seconds total, I told myself to slow down and concentrate. I did, and my throws improved. Wizard was able to make two more catches, and compared to what the other dogs had done up to that point, this was excellent.

The scoring totals announced after that round included Freeflight and Mini-Distance. Wizard and I were in second place, three and a half points behind the first-place team, Gary Gomes and Kelly, but ahead of the two-time world champions, Bill Murphy and Bouncin' Boo. I went back to the hotel and critiqued the contest on video while Wizard cooled down and rested in the air-conditioned room.

The second round of Freeflight took place that evening, and was well attended. I had changed our music from *The Wiz* to the very popular *Ghostbusters* hoping to involve the audience. The crowd not only loved the music, but they loved our routine, too. We hit everything, had no breaks and finished with Wizard catching a long distance throw. We couldn't have done any better given the windy weather conditions and I was quite pleased. The contest was now in the hands of the judges. Gomes, who had been in the lead with Kelly, had as rough of a routine as I had in the first round. Yet, I was prepared for anything, because judging can be so subjective. As the cumulative scores were announced in reverse order from last to first, I held my breath. When I heard everyone else's name but mine, I knew we had caught up. In fact, we were in the lead by a quarter of a point. There was only one final round of Freeflight to go and the two dogs, Wizard and Kelly, were starting in a virtual tie.

A forecasted change in the weather was of some concern to me. There was a chance of rain the next day, in which case the Finals would be cancelled. If this happened, then the current first-place team would be declared the winner. In other words, Wizard and I would be the winners because we were in the lead by a quarter of a point. Although I didn't want to win that way, that night I was finally able to relax. I ate a leisurely dinner and then watched the video of the semi-finals to get psyched for the next day's competition, if indeed,

Peter Bloeme and Wizard competing in the 1984 World Finals at Comiskey Park.

there was going to be one.

For the first time all week I felt calm and had just settled down to bed when the phone rang. It was Alex Stein calling to ask if I would be awake for a few minutes because he wanted to talk. I invited him to come over. My first thought was that there was a mistake in the scoring and I prepared myself for the worst. After 15 minutes had gone by and Stein had not yet arrived, I went to look for him and instead ran into Irv Lander, who asked me if I had gotten the message about a meeting. I told him I hadn't but that Stein had just called me. He told me the officials needed to talk to me in Steve Willett's room (the sponsor's representative). Once there they informed me there had been a mistake in the scoring and instead of my being ahead, I was actually **behind** by a quarter of a point. On the one hand, I was relieved it was nothing worse, but since I was now officially in second place, I started to get nervous. The first thing I did when I got back to the room was call for the latest weather forecast; suddenly it really mattered.

Peter Bloeme and Wizard winning the 1984 World Championships.

After hardly sleeping a wink, I woke to a dark and dreary day. It wasn't raining but looked as if it could at any time. The finals were to take place right before the White Sox game. When we arrived at Comiskey Park, it had gotten a little brighter but was still threatening.

Out of five teams, Wizard and I were set to go fourth, right after Bill Murphy and Bouncin' Boo, who were now in third place. I was glad that we didn't have to perform first or last.

Our turn came and the wind had still not let up; it was swirling at an unsteady 20 miles-per-hour, but luckily the rain was holding off. Wizard started out strong. He hit all the difficult moves, giving me confidence, and we continued to do well. Television and media professionals were on the field during all the routines. They lined up behind second and third base in the outfield. Most of our routine had taken place in left field. When I heard the timekeeper call out *"ten seconds remaining,"* I pointed toward home plate and told Wizard, *"Go"* so that we could finish with what I hoped would be a spectacular long distance throw and catch. Immediately after doing so, I realized that we had been told to stay off the infield, so with hand-signals I redirected Wiz around the media crews to right field. Wizard must have run about 100 yards before catching my 70-yard throw!

It was a great feeling to look up at the large *Diamond Vision* screen and see Wizard and myself 10 times larger than life. No matter what the outcome I was proud of Wizard. Despite his illness, the unfamiliar surroundings and all the attention, he had performed admirably. The final scores were announced. We had received a perfect *"10"* in each of the three rounds of freeflight for teamwork and one *"10"* for difficulty. Not only had I realized my dream of raising and training a world Frisbee dog champion, but I had done it on my first attempt; this was Wizard's first year of competition and now he was the youngest world champion ever.

One hour after the competition ended the skies opened up and it **poured!**

Nancy Mullen of the *Christian Science Monitor* wrote on November 20, 1984:

"At its best, the sport involves a subtle and highly developed interaction between dog and owner. With an impressive routine of hand signals, coordinated moves and precision timing, Peter Bloeme and his dog Wizard won this year's world final of the invitational 'paws' down."

And the *Boston Globe* on September 10, 1984, wrote:

"Leaping lizard, it's Wizard!

"Wizard the wonder dog knows when to quit—he's giving up competitive Frisbee-catching while he's ahead.

"But Wizard and owner Peter Bloeme of New York City went out in style, taking the $1,000 top honors at the Gaines Ashley Whippet Invitational Frisbee-catching tournament Saturday. That, says Bloeme, is nothing to bark at.

"Bloeme, 27, who, himself, tosses the plastic disc toy professionally, has been training and preparing 2-year-old Wizard to be top dog since the border collie was a 4-month-old ball of black and white fur."

Based on my participation in the canine world finals as both competitor and judge, I can honestly say that The Ashley Whippet Invitational is the **premier** Frisbee dog event. All expenses (food, travel and lodging and uniforms, including shirts, shorts, socks, Frisbee discs, carrying bags and beautiful jackets) are provided free. To top off the event a wonderful awards banquet is held. For a competitor who reaches the world finals, no matter how he or she finishes, it is a great achievement and a lifelong memory.

After we won the World Championships I decided to retire Wizard and myself from competition. My reasons for getting involved in the competition in the first place were more to test our ability than anything else. Once we won it was like when I won the Men's World Championships. Once I had reached my dream, I felt that Wizard and I could do a lot more for the sport from the organizational end than as competitors. So we became goodwill ambassadors for the sport. This led to my becoming Deputy Director and now Director of the Friskies Canine Frisbee disc Championships.

Tara jumps for joy at the 1990 Western Regional Championship.

160

Professional Appearances

s a result of each of our world championship titles, Wizard and I have had many exciting opportunities come our way, both separately and together. These have included television appearances on *Late Night with David Letterman*, *Cable News Network (CNN)*, *Good Morning America*, *George Michaels' Sports Machine*, *Steve Allen's The Start of Something Big*, *PBS' Cats & Dogs*, *Live with Regis and Kathie Lee*, *CBS Youth Invitational: Frisbee* and *ESPN*. We've also been featured in articles in *USA Today*, *The New York Post*, *Christian Science Monitor*, *Sports Illustrated*, *Dog World* and *Dog Fancy* along with a host of others. Wizard even performed in the beginning of the Disney movie, *Flight of the Navigator*.

Many years ago, not long after I won the Men's World Frisbee Championships in 1976, I was invited to appear on the nationally televised game show *To Tell the Truth*. As you probably know, each show featured someone who had a unique accomplishment, along with two *impostors* claiming to be that person. The three guests would appear on stage in front of the show's host and a panel of four celebrities. After the announcer read a mini-biography of the guest, the panel would have to figure out through questions and answers who was telling the truth—thus the show's name. During my performance I stumped the panel!

Co-hosts Peter Bloeme and Tom Brookshire during taping of the "CBS Youth Invitational: Frisbee" at Six Flags Over Georgia.

At first I had mixed feelings about being on this particular show because as a 10-year-old I had been watching it when I was told that my father had passed on. However, by appearing on television on that show, I had somehow reconnected with my father because I knew how proud he would have been to see me there. And as a youngster, I never dreamed that someday I would be in that category of *unique* people. So much had happened to put me there.

Part of the fun of what I do entails using my expertise in an advisory capacity. Not long after *To Tell The Truth* I was selected to be the co-host and technical adviser for a 30-minute CBS television special called *CBS Youth Invitational: Frisbee.*

Peter Bloeme with Vin Scully during "Challenge of the Sexes."

My next TV appearance was on *Challenge of the Sexes,* a popular celebrity-type television game show featuring prominent men and women athletes competing against one another. As the current Men's World Frisbee Champion I competed against Monika Lou, the 1976 Women's World Frisbee Champion. I narrowly edged out Lou for the win.

Throughout my professional career I had appeared on many local and national television shows. Yet, there were two that I really wanted to do: *The Johnny Carson Show* and *Late Night with David Letterman,* both on the NBC network. My opportunity finally arose about a year after Wizard won his world title.

Quaker Oats' publicity department told me that Alex Stein had appeared with Ashley Whippet on *Late Night with David Letterman* a couple of years earlier and that the Letterman producers hadn't been pleased with the segment due to Ashley's inability to perform on *stage* in the studio. Ashley's abilities and training were not conducive to performing indoors in a small studio. He was a spectacular outdoor performer who needed a large amount of space. Stein tried to explain this to them before shooting, but they wouldn't listen. He even suggested that they go outside and film something for the show. The result was that the Letterman people weren't keen on having another Frisbee dog on their show.

"*Look, Mr. Bloeme,*" the producer told me, "*we've already had a Frisbee dog on our show and to tell you the truth, he just didn't work out very well. We're sure Wizard, here, is a fine performer, but, with the confines of the studio and all, I'm sure you understand.*"

"*I understand,*" I said. "*Ashley Whippet was a great outdoor performer, but he couldn't do tricks very well indoors. I've trained Wizard to work in small areas. I'm sure if you see some film clips of Wiz, you'll see he CAN perform indoors.*"

"*Fine, kid. We'll take a look.*"

Not long after viewing the tapes of Wizard, the producer called, saying he wanted to see Wizard and me at the studio for an audition. I was thrilled. Wizard wagged his tail. Now, at least we had a chance.

Peter Bloeme and Wizard on "Late Night with David Letterman" with David.

After varied and assorted arrangements, a time and date were set. When we arrived, I noticed a narrow, three-foot red carpet on the floor in the studio. Although I didn't know why it was there, I used it to warm-up Wizard while I waited for the producer, director and some other production people to appear. When they did, my show expertise came out: I performed one of my school shows which included all of Wizard's tricks. Since I trained him with the idea of working in the confines of small areas, he did great.

"Peter, he's wonderful. I must admit, we really didn't think it would work out," the producer said after we had finished our audition. The rest of the production crew echoed their accolades. The only ones on stage who weren't excited and pleased were the stage crew because it turns out, we were using their carpet. Little did they know we would be back.

"Well, Peter, Wizard," the producer said, patting Wiz's head, *"we really liked you both. We will be in touch."* After they were out of earshot, I sighed, saying to Wizard, *"At least we got a tryout and did our best, so we couldn't ask for more."*

That night the phone rang. It was the Letterman show. I crossed my fingers.

"Mr. Bloeme," the producer said.

"Yes?"

"We would like to know if you and your dog are free to do the Letterman show tomorrow night. We had originally hoped New York Yankee's owner George Steinbrenner could do the show, but because of the possibility of the baseball strike, he can't appear. Could you make it?"

"I'd be thrilled to do the show—tomorrow or any day," I said. The timing couldn't have been better because due to their vacation schedule, the show was being taped to be shown two weeks later. That way, I could *wake the kids and phone the neighbors* and let everyone and anyone know about the show in time to tune in.

The show was thrilling for me. Wizard and I were treated first class: They gave us our own dressing room. They had me wear stage makeup. We could have any non-alcoholic drink we wanted. I chose Perrier with a twist of lime. Wizard chose plain water.

Naturally, I was extremely nervous before going on. I mean, it **was** national television and all that. But at the same time I was terribly excited.

Letterman began announcing the show's line-up and got to me, *"And a man who has brought us a dog, his name is Peter...*(look of puzzlement) *pronounce it for me Kevin...*[he asked offstage]...*Peter Bloeme* [correctly pronouncing it Blerm]. *Make a guess how this man spells his name. But you know he has brought an amazing, wonderful, sweet dog who's going to do some unbelievable things for us, that will be Peter Bloeme. And if we have time we will get into his last name a little bit later. Can I show them the last name...*[gets the cue card and shows card]. *Now here is Peter...now say that quietly to yourselves at home..."*

Then he did a skit with the NBC Bookmobile. The routine was going slowly so Letterman said, *"Mr. Bloeme is here tonight."*

"Very exciting," the librarian lady replied.

It continued to go slowly.

"Maybe it's time to bring out Mr. Bloeme," quipped Letterman.

There were three guests on the show that night and I was the second, after Dr. Ruth Westheimer, the famous sex therapist and psychologist.

The diminutive Westheimer was talking about her new sex game in her unmistakable accent.

Letterman interrupted, *"Let me ask you something. Does the word Bloeme appear anywhere in the..."*

Westheimer replied, *"No but it just may...I'll tell you why I did this..."*

"Very nice man, got a great dog too, really sweet dog," Letterman continued.

"Let's talk about sex not dogs," Westheimer said a little testily.

After a commercial break Wiz and I ran out on stage. The studio audience had been treated to a song by the band, which was excellent, but very loud. Since I was already nervous back stage, I wondered if their playing would affect Wizard.

When Letterman introduced us, we came out as though we were at a professional sporting event.

Peter Bloeme and Wizard with Steve Allen during taping of the show, "The Start of Something Big."

JACKIE BERNARD

Letterman, a consummate dog lover, kept petting Wizard and saying what a beautiful animal he was.

"Now, then, what are you going to have Wizard do?"

He really seemed to enjoy Wizard's performance. It's tough working indoors on a small carpet, but we managed to get in many interesting tricks. The catapult was by far his best. The camera man had missed it and my friends in the studio audience told me later on they had seen him wince in disappointment.

We ended with Wizard taking the Frisbee out of Letterman's mouth At least, that's what was supposed to have happened. Letterman put it in his mouth and then quickly took it out complaining that it tasted like Gaines Burgers which got a big laugh. Then, in spite of my warnings, Letterman didn't let go of the Frisbee in time, so it was more of a collision. He may very well have planned it that way. It looked great on instant replay.

Letterman was wonderful to work with. He truly enjoyed Wizard and the segment. What may surprise people about appearing on a show like Letterman is that he doesn't meet with the guests before the taping. The producer told me that is because he wants the exchange with the guests to be fresh. After the show, Letterman came over to us, and shook my hand and Wizard's paw.

"Peter, Wiz," he said, patting Wiz's head, *"very impressive showing. He's a great dog."*

My only regret was not having a chance to ask David what his top ten things to do with a used dog disc were.

Many of the films I've appeared in were never released to the general public because they were "industrials," private films used for industries or companies. One of the most interesting industrial film projects I participated in was *Sea Dream,* a three-dimensional film for Marineland in St. Augustine, Florida.

It all started innocently enough. *"Mr. Bloeme?"* a voice on the other end of my phone asked hesitantly, having difficulty, as usual, pronouncing my name. *"My name is Murray Lerner. I'm a film producer and director and I'm looking for someone who can throw a Frisbee. Wham-O told me you're the man for me. Do you think you're accurate enough to throw a Frisbee directly at a camera for some special effects in a film I'm doing?"*

"What? Was he kidding?," I asked myself.

"Mr. Lerner, I am the world accuracy champion and a Frisbee professional. If a disc can be thrown accurately at a camera, I can do it,"

I replied as modestly as possible.

The filming took place on Marineland's beach in St. Augustine, Florida. Once the shot was set up, it dawned on me why Lerner had to have someone extremely accurate. He wanted a Frisbee thrown directly at the camera to invoke the full 3-D effect. To protect his equipment, he had a large Plexiglass sheet set up in front of it. All I had to do, from 20 yards away on a windy beach, was to throw and hit a spot three inches high by six inches wide. To make matters even more difficult, he was filming in slow motion. That meant I'd have three tries for every large reel of film. Filming in slow motion requires the film to travel faster than normal through the camera. Each miss would add to the cost of the filming and compound the pressure on me. To save on film, I practiced a lot and each time I thought I was doing well, Lerner would tell me to throw closer to the center of the lens! By noon he felt we had some good *takes in the can* (film talk for film already shot), so we went on to some easier beach scenes.

The next day we watched the *rushes* (more film talk meaning scenes shot the day before) and they were very dramatic! The Frisbee looked as if it were floating out off the screen and over the audience. The results pleased Lerner, but we still had another day to fill some spots.

Between takes, I threw some boomerang throws out over the water. I joked to a friend as I let one fly, *"Hey, P.J., watch. I bet Lerner will want me to do these throws on camera!"*

"As a matter of fact..." he said, coming up behind me. He not only wanted the throw on camera, but right at the camera.

Every time I made a good arching throw, the camera man lost sight of it. It seemed that when the camera man followed it, I would make a bad throw until finally, I threw one he followed perfectly. It actually landed right on top of the camera!

Although my part in the total film was small, it added

1990 World Runner-up Bill Watters making his now famous Miller Lite pitch. Wizard, by the way was the "other" dog in one version of the commercial.

quite a bit of zest. The film opens with a scene of P.J. and me playing Frisbee on the beach. Because of the 3-D effects, one of my throws to P.J. looks like it goes right over the audience.

After showing the two of us playing for a while, the camera slowly pans out into the sea for some exciting underwater shots, constantly taking advantage of the 3-D effects and then ends with a shot of a dolphin catching a Frisbee. Marineland even built a special million dollar theater to show it in.

I did manage to see the show once. *"Excuse me, ladies and gentleman,"* a voice came over the speakers as the lights came on in the theater after the showing, *"but we have in our audience the man who performed the Frisbee scenes—Peter Bloeme. Peter, take a bow."* Well, if you insist, I thought, loving every minute of applause and the autographs. Show biz.

While films and TV shows are great for the resumé, television commercials are great for the pocketbook. They pay well and don't take much time. You're paid according to union rules based on how often you appear and how often the commercial is aired on television. One of the best-known commercials I did was for Pepsi-Cola. I arrived for the shoot, hoping I might get a good-sized part, and it looked as though I would when the director told me he wanted me to drink some Pepsi-Cola on camera.

"Drink it without stopping. The entire bottle," I was told.

"Give me a break. How often do real people do that?," I thought.

"I hope you're thirsty," the director said as he walked away.

I wasn't.

There were two extras on the sidelines that were supposed to work with me on the shot. One was a girl who was supposed to hug me and pat me on the back like she was my girlfriend, while the other, a guy, was to wring a sponge out over my head to cool me off.

"And, action!," the director yelled.

I did my bit, running off to the sidelines. The girlfriend hugged me and the sponger started his bit.

"Yea, yea," she yelled. I was trying to drink this Pepsi-Cola all at once, she's thumping me on the back and the guy with the sponge, instead of wringing it over my head, hits me with it. This, in turn, caused my front teeth to knock into the bottle. Great. I'm gasping for breath, trying not to vomit and chipping my front teeth. All on film.

It took a while, but they finally had mercy on me and we ended with some good (safe) *refreshing* takes.

I obtained a good deal of satisfaction, though, as the final edit featured a move I call the windmill. I jump, spin in the air and catch the Frisbee between my legs with my hand in an upside-down position and land on my feet. Simply put, it's a move that resembles a flying-spinning-reverse-between-the-legs catch.

One of the most unusual requests I ever received was from a filmmaker under contract with the United States Government. It seems that the U.S. Government, in the days before CNN, put together a film each month on American happenings, similar in format to *Evening Magazine*. Each film consisted of different segments on business, art, sports—whatever. The filmmaker wanted to do the sports segment on Frisbee with Monika Lou, the 1976 Woman's World Champion and me. We got together for the shoot in San Francisco.

To the best of my knowledge, the film was designed for propaganda purposes, glorifying one *positive* side of the United States. I still don't know where, or how, it was ever used.

My exposure has not only been domestic, but I have also done many performances for international concerns. In the years since Alex Stein burst upon the scene at Dodger Stadium, the Ashley Whippet Celebrity Team has made quite an impact on the sporting world, including an appearance at Super Bowl XII. Because of this, we were invited by the NFL brass to an international event that made me feel as if we were a part of history—an NFL exhibition game in Berlin, Germany. Wizard and I joined Alex Stein with Ashley Whippet Jr. and Jeff Perry with Gilbert in performing before, between quarters and after the game at the American Bowl between the Los Angeles Rams and Kansas City Chiefs. After traveling to New York, Perry and I rendezvoused with Stein, who came in from Cleveland. From there we flew to Europe, transferred in Frankfurt and caught one final flight for Berlin.

What made this even more special was that this was at the time that the Berlin Wall came down.

Each time we boarded our aircraft enroute, we made sure the dogs had made the connection. We all were a little concerned about the long flight's effect on them because it was about 15 hours total for the dogs to spend in their kennels. Still, we would have been more concerned if they hadn't gotten on the correct flights. As it turned out when we claimed them in Berlin, they were all fine and eager to go.

We arrived on a Thursday morning, did the game Saturday and left Monday morning. Despite several required appearances during our visit, we managed to have a **great** time. We went out each night and were able to experience German food and the night life.

The game took place Saturday, August 11, 1990 at 7:30 p.m. German time, at the Olympic Stadium (the home of the 1936 Olympic Games). Before the game there was a tremendous tailgate party on the grounds.

Judging by the wild cheers, one would think that the crowd of 55,000 appreciated our performances even more than the game. During most of the play the spectators appeared more intent on doing the wave than paying attention to the game. This might have been because it was an early exhibition contest and there was not an abundance of action on the field as the August 20, 1990 issue of *Sports Illustrated* said:

"On one of the fields the Frisbee dogs drew a bigger crowd than the subsequent practice game between the Dusseldorf Panthers and the Berlin Eagles [two local clubs]."

First International Ambassadog Tour, Jeff Perry & Gilbert; Alex Stein & Ashley Whippet Jr.; & Peter Bloeme & Wizard in Berlin, Germany.

Sunday was our last day, and we made the most of it by tearing down some of the Berlin Wall, which was all the rage at the time. Airport security people looked at us strangely at every stop on the flight back because of all the cement we had in our bags.

The flight back was faster and easier on the dogs since we went non-stop from Berlin to New York. After clearing customs in New York we were able to take the dogs out for a few minutes before checking them back in for their last leg of the trip.

I once heard a story about a world finalist who said that upon taking off in a plane, he heard his dog barking through the cabin floor. He banged on the floor to try to quiet him down. I thought it was a cute story but secretly wondered whether it was true—until our flight from New York to Atlanta. Jeff Perry and I were in first class. The plane had started to push back from the terminal when it stopped to pick up some more baggage. It appeared as if more pets were loaded at the last second. We heard a bark, then a pause, then a bark then a pause, etc. Embarrassed, I recognized that unmistakable bark pattern as Wizard's. It took me a moment to figure out what had happened, but then it dawned on me that they must have put a cat next to Wizard's kennel. You may recall that Wizard thinks of cats as self-propelled Frisbee discs. So, naturally he barks to get them to move. Unfortunately, there was no place for either the cat or Wizard to go, so he just kept barking. To my relief, once we took off, the engines drowned out the sound. Perry, however, gave me grief the whole way home.

Of all the possible venues for showcasing Frisbee dogs, there is nothing better then a sporting event. We have done demonstrations during football, baseball, horse racing, soccer and many other games. Because of Wizard's skills, my favorite are basketball games.

There is nothing to compare with performing during the halftime of a NBA (National Basketball Association) game. I arrive early as the crowd starts to gather. The arena has a certain electricity to it. The artificial lights are ablaze and the music builds slowly with intensity. The building takes on life, the pace quickens, the crowd starts to buzz and the teams begin their warm-up. I watch all this from a corner, keenly aware of all that's going on around me: Children look for autographs, couples converse and anticipation grows. Reality sets in as the world of advertising rears its not-so-subtle head and screams out the Budweiser message. It is announced that anyone caught throwing anything in the arena will be ejected. I glance down at Wizard.

It's funny, but a sellout crowd indoors in Charlotte, North Carolina, of over 24,000 Hornets' fans can be more intimidating than a sellout crowd in the Dallas Cowboys football stadium. What makes it different and more

Japanese television star Iyo Matsumoto with Peter Bloeme and Wizard.

171

exciting is that the floor is like a stage and the audience is close enough to see and be seen. The arena captures the cheers and boos and magnifies them 100%. To me, it's the perfect venue to display Wizard's intelligence, quickness and coordination.

The tension (for me) starts building when the first quarter ends. I start warming up and check on Wizard from time-to-time to ensure he's resting comfortably in the locker room. With about

Artistic Japanese photo of Magic in the mud and snow with Mt. Fuji in the background.

five minutes left before halftime, I start getting nervous and put Wizard's custom-made shoes on him (so he won't slip on the floor). Time begins to drag; the last few minutes seem to take forever. Finally, with one minute to go, Wizard and I are perched at the corner of the court. The buzzer goes off, my introduction begins and I tune everything out while Wizard goes nuts. After one of our basketball shows, a sportswriter reported:

"How good was Jordan? Put it this way: Wizard the wonder dog, the world famous canine who entertained the fans at half with tremendous leaps for the Frisbee, was seen afterward taking notes from [Michael] Jordan as to the art of sky-walking."

Many projects I have been involved in had great potential, but for one reason or another they didn't come off. The music video *Top Dog* was one of them. One day I received a message on my answering machine from a television and film agent, named Robby Kass. He said he wanted to talk about two of his clients, David Wasson and Joe Karioth, who are screenwriters, songwriters, actors, musicians and singers. They were in the process of writing a song called *Top Dog* and he had mentioned my name to them because of Wizard. *"Are you interested in speaking to them about doing a music video to go along with their song?"* he asked. I said of course, so he gave me their telephone number. I called, not knowing what to expect. David sounded excited as I told him about Wizard and myself and I told him I would send him a videotape of us in action to give him and his partner a realistic image of what to expect.

They told me that once they viewed the tape, they went back and rewrote the song. They couldn't believe what Wizard and I could do. Plus, it was now easier for them to write because they had visuals they could work with.

A few weeks later, I met with Wasson, Karioth and their producer, Maggie Simon. Over dinner, we discussed different ideas about funding and locations for the video. By then they were fully aware of Wizard and my capabilities, while I had no way of knowing theirs. They invited me to the taping on Friday. When I arrived at the studio, I met the musicians—Bob the bass player, who had his Masters degree in music, Arnie a professional jazz drummer, Bobby the lead guitarist and Joie Gallo, the lead singer.

Top Dog sounded great. I had shown them some photos of Wizard in action and they were psyched. They ran through it a few times with Wasson making suggestions to Gallo on different techniques for the song—where to be clean, raspy, adjust pace, etc. It kept sounding better and better. Once the voice track was finalized, it was Bobby, the lead guitarist's, turn. Bobby, who looks like Jay Leno's twin, started by laying down one lead track, then another and finally a third, so that he was jamming with himself. He did a great job and sounded fantastic! I was amazed at how fast the whole thing came together.

By the end of the evening, the basic song was done. A song was written, recorded and produced for Wizard. I was excited! Unfortunately, as many great and exciting projects sometimes do, this one hasn't yet gone anywhere. Here is *Top Dog* by David Wasson and Joe Karioth:

> *"The streets are cold and filled with pain, That's no place for a stranger, You're just a face without a name, Always looking at danger, Never found the time to ask yourself why, You learn the rules, then they change the game, No one wants a beginner, You've got the stuff to make your name, You're the best. You're the winner, Just want a chance to get up and fly*
>
> *"You can be the top dog, You can be the one to lead the pack, You can be the top dog, No time for sitting still or lookin' back, (cause) you can be the top dog, You can be the one to set the beat, You can be the top dog, You're the one to take the heat*
>
> *"(You're running hard and breathin' fast), You're*

runnin' low and near the end, Almost ready to give in,
You were reachin' out and you found a friend, This is it.
Now you're livin', All you need is just a little more time"

It is important to have professional goals. My latest professional goal is to further the sport of Canine Frisbee throughout the world. To this end I wrote this book. Since the first edition of *Frisbee Dogs,* I have produced a 30 minute companion training video called *Frisbee Dogs: Training Video.* Both have received enthusiastic reviews and responses in the media and garnered sales throughout the world.

Through the years, I've been featured on television many times in other countries including France, Canada and Japan. After a number of successful appearances on Japanese television, I was contacted by some enthusiasts from Japan who were interested in attending a personal clinic. I arranged for them to attend a Regional competition and took advantage of their time in the U.S. to work with them on throwing and the basics of training their dogs. It was a bit unusual because they didn't actually bring their dogs so we faked it, but they all had a great time and learned a lot.

Canine Frisbee is a relatively new sport in Japan. Its burgeoning popularity, coupled with our successful sponsorship agreement with Friskies PetCare Products in the U.S., resulted in our first Ambassadog trip to Japan in 1993. Our assignment was to film a dog food commercial for the Japanese brand. Unfortunately, celebrity touring team members Gilbert and Magic weren't invited because the commercial's producer insisted upon featuring a brown dog using a black background. In this day of computerization and colorization, you'd think Magic or Gilbert could simply be *morphed and electronically adjusted,* but this was, unfortunately, not the case.

Actually we needed two brown dogs that looked alike so I selected celebrity touring team member Eldon McIntire and Cricket along with Regional finalist Richard Munger and Ginger for the assignment. The producer was in for a treat, because not

Frisbee Dogs: Training Video, comes complete with a doggy diploma.

only do Ginger and Cricket look alike, but Richard and Eldon do too!

It was a long and grueling trip. In addition to serving as the technical advisor for the commercial, I made numerous media appearances and participated in the filming of an in-store promotional video.

Upon our return home, I had high hopes that the

Richard Munger, Ginger, Peter Bloeme, Cricket and Eldon McIntire in Furano Japan for Friskies television commercial.

sport would catch on further in Japan, but I wasn't sure how long it would take. Well, it didn't take long. Just a few months later I received a call from Fuji Television, Japan's largest network, inviting me to return to Japan to participate in the filming of a special program to celebrate the beginning of the year of the dog. This time Jeff Perry and Gilbert and my dog Magic and I made the long trek to Japan. We were to put on clinics, exhibitions and supervise a New Year's special competition for the network.

By this time, the Friskies Frisbee dog commercial was airing throughout select markets in Japan. However, I had no idea of the enormous popularity this sport would achieve almost overnight. My first clue came when more than 60 dog/human teams registered for our first clinic! Some even had copies of my book and video, some had attended my clinic in the U.S., but all were equally enthusiastic. To set the proper tone I began by explaining through an interpreter my feelings on the sport and the direction I would like to see it take in Japan. The Mini-Distance competition was spirited and reminded me of the early days here in the U.S. We selected the top 30 competitors for the televised finals a week later.

Jeff Perry and Peter Bloeme in their Japanese summerwear.

When I heard it was going to be televised, I expected the usual two camera set-up we see at the World Finals with additional crews representing the networks. Boy, was I wrong. There were a total of seven cameras positioned at all angles to cover the Mini-Distance event!

As the production crews were setting up, I noticed a blimp hovering nearby and kidded to Perry that Fuji even hired the *Goodyear* blimp to cover the event. We enjoyed a good chuckle over that comment. Later I found out that the blimp overhead **had** been hired by Fuji Television for the shoot!

The enthusiasm of the Japanese competitors was refreshing and I look forward to the continued sport's development worldwide.

1992 World Runner-ups Greg Tresan & Jumpin' Jess fall head over heels for the sport.

Afterword

With this second edition of *Frisbee Dogs* just a few weeks away from publication there are a few words I'd like to add.

In the last few years there has been a tremendous increase in the popularity of canine Frisbee. This increased interest has resulted in a number of television and print campaigns providing even greater recognition. As the sport grows, more dog and disc clubs will be founded, more people will get involved, and dogs all over will enjoy the benefits.

However, the positive media exposure will continue only if those performers in the public eye temper their enthusiasm and keep their egos under control. At all times competitors and performers must continue to give back to the sport, and represent it in a respectful, unselfish, positive and professional manner.

One of the most positive directions the sport is taking is in the development of dog and disc clubs. These clubs provide a not-for-profit forum for practitioners of the sport at a *grass roots* level. They provide an opportunity for shared insights with people who have the same interests, give demonstrations to entertain varied audiences including schools and charities, and finally, perpetuate the sport by attracting new members. Clubs not only promote competition, but friendship and sportsmanship, too.

I am very pleased by the

interest and success the sport is enjoying. However, I am concerned that some people will enter the sport for the wrong reasons. Sadly, I have seen the human side of disc competition go in this direction.

There has always been a conscious effort by the founders of the sport to keep the value of prizes at a minimum. It was always felt that as the prizes grew in value, you would see a proportional decline in sportsmanship. The sport was developed with fun, camaraderie, and responsible pet ownership as the key motivators.

It is my sincere hope that this book will encourage you to become more involved in the exciting and rewarding sport of canine Frisbee. I am certain that your dog will love you for it. Good luck and I hope to see you and your dog out in the park enjoying the sport!

*Top to bottom, left to right: Cody, Omar, Hyper Hank, Gilbert, Enthisiastic Pair,
China, Sparky, Magic, Casey and Scout.*

Appendix

Contest Information

Canine Frisbee Championships
4060-D Peachtree Road, Suite 326
Atlanta, GA 30319
(800) 786-9240

Equipment and Supplies

Flying Dog Products
4060-D Peachtree Road, Suite 326
Atlanta, GA 30319
(800) 786-9240
Products include: *Frisbee Dogs: Training Video, Frisbee Dogs: How to Raise, Train & Compete (this book)*, practice discs, posters, bumper stickers, disc towels, key chains, water bottles, T-shirts and more.

Recommended Reading

The Art of Raising a Puppy
by The Monks of New Skete
Little, Brown and Company
Boston, Toronto, London

Athletes: Photographs 1960-1986
Edited by Ruth Silverman
Alfred A. Knopf
New York, NY

Dog Fancy Magazine
P.O. Box 53264
Boulder, CO 80322

Dog World Magazine
29 North Wacker Drive
Chicago, IL 60606

Dogs on Duty
by Catherine O'Neill
National Geographic Society
Washington, D.C.

Dr. Pitcairn's Complete Guide to "Natural Health for Dogs and Cats"
by Richard H. Pitcairn, D.V.M, Ph. D, and Susan Hubbie Pitcairn
Rodale Press, Inc.
33 East Minor Street
Emmaus, PA 18049

Frisbee Players Handbook
by Mark Danna & Dan Poynter
Parachuting Publications
P.O. Box 4232
Santa Barbara, CA 93103

Friskies Training Manual (free)
by Irv Lander
4060-D Peachtree Rd, Ste 326
Atlanta, GA 30319
800-786-9240

The Koehler Method of Dog Training
by William Koehler
Howell Book House
866 Third Avenue
New York, NY 10022

How to be Your Dog's Best Friend a Training Manual for Dog Owners
by The Monks of New Skete
Little, Brown and Company
Boston, Toronto, London

Paul Loeb's Complete Book of Dog Training
by Paul Loeb
Prentice-Hall
Englewood Cliffs, NJ

Simon & Schuster's Guide To Dogs
Edited by Elizabeth Meriwether Schuler
Simon & Schuster, Inc.
1230 Avenue of the Americas
New York, New York 10020

Super-Training Your Dog
by Jo and Paul Loeb
Prentice-Hall
Englewood Cliffs, NJ

Traveling With Towser
Gaines TWT
P.O. Box 1007
Kankakee, Il 60902

Index